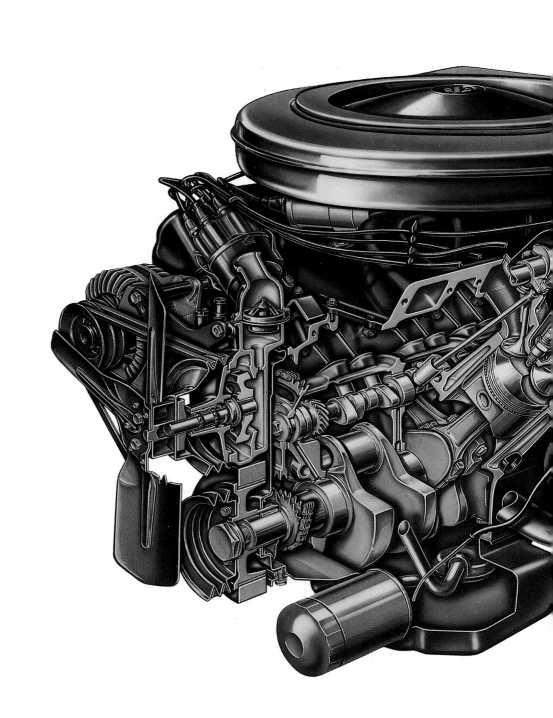

Motorbooks International

MUSCLE CAR COLOR HISTORY

HEMI

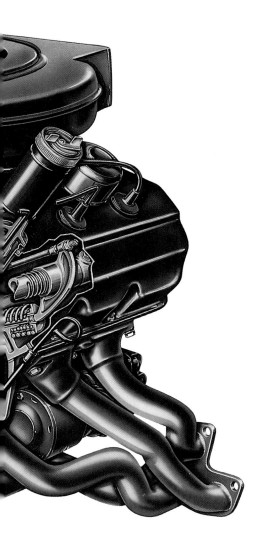

Anthony Young

First published in 1991 by Motorbooks International Publishers & Wholesalers, P O Box 2, 729 Prospect Avenue, Osceola, WI 54020 USA

Motorbooks International books are also available at discounts in bulk quantity for industrial or sales-promotional use. For details write to Special Sales Manager at the Publisher's address

Library of Congress Cataloging-in-Publication Data
Young, Anthony.
    Hemi: history of the Chrysler Hemi V-8 engine / Anthony Young.
        p.   cm. — (Motorbooks International muscle car color histories)
    Includes index.
    ISBN 0-87938-537-5
    1. Chrysler automobile—Motors—History. I. Title. II. Series.
TL215.C55Y67 1991
629.25'04—dc20   91–11015

Printed in Singapore by PH Productions

On the front cover: *The 1970 Hemi Charger R/T was one of the most exciting Mopar cars to ever wear the 426 Hemi badge.* Musclecar Reviews

On the back cover: *Sixteen years of Hemi lore.*

On the frontispiece: *Dodge named its fresh air induction system after its famous factory drag-racing team, the Ramchargers. This setup, shown on the 1970 Coronet R/T, fed the 426 Hemi below. Note the 426 with the Hemi on the air-cleaner cover.* David Gooley

On the title page: *Assembly layout drawing for one of the first-generation Hemis, the DeSoto FireDome V-8.* Chrysler

Contents

Acknowledgments

Thanks to the willingness and cooperation of all I spoke with at Chrysler Corporation, the Chrysler Hemi story has finally been told.

I want to thank John Wehrly for arranging the interviews, and Rose Mueller for her deft handling of appointments. Bruce Raymond produced a great deal of printed matter for me on the 426 Hemi, and got the ball rolling for the all-important photographs.

Special thanks go to Bill Weertman. He not only gave me a great deal of heretofore unknown information on the 426 Hemi's initial development, he also told me where I could reach other engineers who contributed to both the first- and second-generation Hemi V–8s. I obtained the majority of black-and-white photos in the book through him. I also received from him copies of SAE papers, memos and other documents, giving me valuable information. His

This 1970 Dodge Coronet R/T with the optional 426 Hemi is one of only a few examples in existence today. Fewer than fifteen were originally built. This kind of rarity ensures its collector value. This car is owned by Ken Funk of Los Angeles, California. David Gooley

careful editing of each chapter and comments helped to make this history accurate and more than just a story.

Contributing their recollections for chapter one were Bill Drinkard, Everett Moeller, Harold Welch, Fred Shrimpton, Robert Cahill, Bert Bouwkamp, Tom Hoover and Troy Simonsen.

Tom Hoover also offered a wealth of information for chapter two, as did Bill Weertman. Bob Rarey, Dick Maxwell, Brian Schram, Steve Baker, Ted Flack, Troy Simonsen, John Wehrly, Bob Tarrozi and Dan Mancini all contributed to the chapter also. Dick Landy loaned me some rare photos of the 426 Hemi cars he raced, and some great background on his winning A/FX car.

For chapter three on the street 426 Hemi, I must again thank Bill Weertman for all the documents he offered me from his files that helped me trace the creation of these mightiest of Mopars. Ted Flack, Oscar Willard, Bert Bouwkamp and Tom Hoover gave their input to the chapter also.

Kathy Donovan was most helpful in supplying me information on her husband's work on the first aluminum-block Hemi, the Donovan 417, recalled in chapter four. Keith Black was generous with his time in telling me how he

got into the engine-building business, and how the Keith Black aluminum 426 Hemi block came to be. His secretary Judy Rodriguez made sure I received the KB literature and photos. Larry Shepard at Chrysler's Mopar Performance division not only contributed to chapter four, but also offered constructive criticism on the other chapters in the book, as he did with my first book, *Mighty Mopars*.

The assistance of Barbara Fronczak and her staff at the Chrysler Information Resources Center was also appreciated.

I would like to thank the editors of *Automobile Quarterly* in granting me permission to use material from my 1984 article, "HEMI—Four Letters for Performance," that appeared in Volume 22, Number 2.

The idea for this book must really go to my editor at Motorbooks International, Michael Dregni. It was he who called me at work one day and asked if I would be interested in writing a book on the Chrysler Hemi V–8 engines. Silly question, Mike.

Finally, I want to thank my wife Annie for her encouragement while writing this book. The dream is coming true.

Dodge "426"
Hemi-charger V-8

DODGE DIVISION CHRYSLER MOTORS CORPORATION

Introduction

A New Era of Performance

The first-generation Hemi V–8 of the 1950s and the 426 Hemi of the 1960s built by Chrysler Corporation are among the most significant automotive engine designs of the twentieth century. They broke new ground in terms of performance for their day.

The performance era might have taken longer to arrive had not the Chrysler FirePower, Dodge Red Ram and DeSoto FireDome V–8s made their appearance. It has been said that these Hemi-head engines launched the horsepower wars by forcing General Motors and Ford to match their performance. While output was initially modest compared to what came later, the real proof of the first-generation Chrysler Hemi's performance potential was achieved with its tire test car.

This car, a Kurtis Kraft rear-engine design with a modified 331 ci FirePower V–8, put out roughly 400 hp and developed a top speed of over 180 mph. Its performance surpassed that of the Indy cars themselves. It was so fast, the rulebook was rewritten before Chrysler could enter one in the Indianapolis 500.

Enthusiasts could still experience that feeling of power with the advent of the Chrysler 300 in 1955. During the 1930s, the mighty Duesenberg J and SJ cars were the fastest on the road; lesser

Hemi graphics went from mild to wild, above. By 1971, huge, billboard-size graphics covered the rear quarter panels on the Hemi 'Cuda. Left, this display engine of the 426 drag Hemi with its cutaway parts drew crowds at SAE conventions and car shows. Dodge called its version the 426 Hemi-Charger V–8. David Gooley; Chrysler

cars had no choice but to get out of the way. The Depression was the death knell of the Duesenberg and other performance marques, and it wasn't until the Chrysler 300 appeared that auto enthusiasts once again witnessed a similar

quantum leap in automobile engine performance.

With its 300 hp 331 ci FirePower Hemi-head V–8, nothing could touch a Chrysler 300 in terms of acceleration or top speed. More than a few men thought of the ways to scrape together the money—somehow—to buy that gleaming red Chrysler 300 they stared longingly at through the showroom window. Whenever one was parked on the street, it always drew a crowd.

Suddenly, Chrysler was a name to be reckoned with in stock-car racing. Chrysler 300s were the cars to beat, and they truly were stock cars in those days. The racing success only lent more prestige to the 300s on the Chrysler showroom floors across America.

The recession of 1957 had a stunning effect on car sales. Compared to 1956, sales of DeSotos plunged fifty-four percent and Dodge sales were off forty-seven percent; the story was pretty much the same for every manufacturer. Chrysler had been working on a new, more economical Wedge-head engine family to replace its Hemi V–8s and the recession added impetus. Quietly, the Hemis disappeared from the Dodge, DeSoto and Chrysler line of cars.

The engines, however, were discovered by hot rodders. The 392 Chrysler

FirePower was the Hemi of choice, and the intercorporate Dodge Ramchargers were the first to capitalize on the Hemi's power on the quarter-mile strip. These engines found their way into boats as well. Keith Black made a name for himself modifying these engines for racing boats off the coast of California before moving on to Hemi-powered cars.

In the early sixties, Chrysler had shown it could truly build high-performance engines for the quarter-mile strip with its Max Wedge 413 and 426 V-8s. Stock-car racing was another matter, as the Wedge-head engines had a more difficult time. A corporate decision was made to design and build a new racing engine that would reign supreme on both the track and the strip. That engine would become the 426 Hemi V-8.

This new Hemi V-8 borrowed the lessons learned from the first-generation Hemi and with incredible speed, Chrysler unveiled its new engine at the 1964 Daytona 500 with spectacular results. During the sixties, Ford and GM waged war with Hemi-powered Dodges and Plymouths.

It can honestly be said the 426 Hemi drag engine experienced even greater success than its circle-track counterpart. Regardless of class, the 426 Hemi was king—from Super Stock to Top Fuel Eliminator. The inherent strength and extraordinary breathing ability of the 426 Hemi enabled the horsepower levels to be dialed in. How fast you wanted to go was limited only by money, and only the 426 Hemi was capable of delivering the horsepower levels to drop elapsed times from ten seconds to nine, then eight, seven, finally into the sixes, and even lower. As ETs (elapsed times) went down, horsepower shot up, with the most powerful Hemis now generating close to 4000 hp!

While the circle-track Hemis raced for less than a decade, the Chrysler Hemi has continued to prosper on the quarter-mile ever since its inception. The drag-racing Hemis found their way into wild factory cars like the altered-wheelbase AF/X cars of 1965 and the Super Stock Darts and Barracudas of 1968. Once Chrysler ceased production of the drag Hemi, drag racers continued to use the 426 Hemi with such enthusiasm, engine builders came forward to fill the void.

The 426 street Hemi, of course, was one of the most respected engines of the muscle-car era. Having only the most rudimentary changes necessary to make it streetable, the 426 street Hemi carried with it a level of prestige no other engine could match. Many of these Hemi-powered cars spent much of their time at the strip, and that was the idea!

The collectibility of these 426 Hemi-powered Dodges and Plymouths was dormant for more than a decade after the street Hemi ceased production with the 1971 model year. For performance enthusiasts, the latter seventies were depressing. It was obvious that high-output engines from the car manufacturers were gone forever. These enthusiasts began looking around for used muscle cars, and the most desirable among them had the 426 Hemi. In the early eighties, it was still possible to pick up a 426 street Hemi Mopar for $10,000 or so. Prices began rising rapidly in the late eighties. These Hemi-powered Mopars were destined to become the most collectible—and expensive—cars from the supercar era. Some of the rarer examples are offered for sale in excess of $100,000.

With the continuing popularity of the 426 Hemi at the drag strip, many of the old iron-block Hemis were finally wearing out with replacements hard to find. In 1990, Mopar Performance—the performance parts division of Chrysler Corporation formerly known as Direct Connection—announced plans to re-tool a new 426 Hemi iron block and cylinder heads to fill the needs of aftermarket enthusiasts.

In this book you will read about these engines—how they were conceived, designed, built, tested and raced. To give a truly comprehensive racing history of Chrysler's Hemi V-8s, however, is really beyond the scope of this book. Many of the key designers, engineers and technicians of both the first-generation Hemi and the 426 Hemi were interviewed, and their comments are used extensively.

To all the Chrysler Hemi enthusiasts around the world, this book is for you.

Hemi 'Cudas were rare, and rarer still were the 1970 Hemi 'Cuda convertibles. This was the first year the Barracuda was available with the 426 street Hemi. Stuffing a 426 Hemi into a 'Cuda convertible resulted in what is today the most collectible combination. Musclecar Review

FirePower, FireDome & Red Ram

First-Generation Hemi Engines 1951–1958

K. T. Keller said, "Bill, I think maybe you've got the
right plan." That was the thing that turned the
whole thing around.

—William E. Drinkard

World War II had a pervasive effect on the corporations of America. Practically every type of company manufacturing consumer goods halted production to take on military contracts. The automobile companies were no different; the automotive assembly lines were shut down to make way for what came to be known as the arsenal of democracy.

In January 1942, Chrysler Corporation shut down its Dodge, Plymouth, Chrysler, DeSoto and Imperial assembly plants and began the massive conversion to manufacturing war materiel. With amazing speed, Chrysler tooled up and began building wings for bombers, tanks, anti-aircraft guns, parts for ships and aircraft, as well as jeeps and trucks. From the crucible of this effort came the genesis of the idea for what would become the Chrysler hemispherical-combustion-chamber V–8 engine.

With the end of the war, Chrysler slowly resumed passenger car production in the closing months of 1945. Like the other auto makers, it looked to the postwar economy with promise. Work was begun on new engine designs as a means of getting more power and smoother performance. In a real sense, the engine that finally emerged represented the forthcoming power, prestige

On the DeSoto, above, the Hemi V–8 under the hood was announced with a medallion mounted to the fuel-filler door on the right side, as well as the left rear fender. Left, the Chrysler 300 of 1955 instantly became the most powerful American production car on the road. Musclecar Review; David Gooley

and prosperity of postwar America.

Two areas were felt to hold the most promise in improving engine performance: compression ratio and volumetric efficiency. Boosting compression was an old horsepower trick, but the ability to do so was dependent on the octane rating of available pump-grade fuel. Efforts to increase octane rating of gasoline after World War II were slow, and this limited engineering in the area of higher compression ratios for cars.

Volumetric efficiency was a product of combustion-chamber design specifically and engine breathing in general. Chrysler decided on a concurrent design and engineering program to evaluate compression ratios and combustion-chamber designs as a means of boosting power.

Hemi Research and Development

Chrysler used a unique single-cylinder engine to evaluate cylinder head designs with a compression ratio of 7.0:1. The familiar L-head and F-head were tested, as well as a conventional valve-in-head design and a hemispherical cylinder head. Chrysler had practical reasons for wanting an improved cylinder-head design. Combustion-chamber deposits could significantly reduce power over a given period. These depos-

The first application of the Chrysler hemispherical-combustion-chamber cylinder head in a passenger car was on this straight-six prototype engine. Chrysler

The straight-six Hemi-head prototype engine allowed Chrysler engineers to confirm the cylinder head's performance before tooling up for the prototype V-8. These photos show the juxtaposition of the intake and exhaust valves and double rocker shafts. Chrysler

its affected thermal and volumetric efficiencies, resulting in power losses of as much as ten percent after only 5,000 to 10,000 miles. A combustion chamber with a low surface-to-volume ratio minimized these losses. All indicators were pointing to a hemispherical combustion chamber, which inherently had a high thermal and volumetric efficiency as well as low surface-to-volume ratio.

Hemispherical combustion chambers were really nothing new. One of the first, if not *the* first, uses of the Hemi head was on the 1904 four-cylinder Welch passenger-car engine. The Hemi head was the design of choice for such famous racing marques as Duesenberg, Stutz, Miller and Offenhauser.

The fledgling aircraft engine industry seized upon the hemispherical cylinder head as the best power-producing design for air-cooled engines. In fact, during World War II, Chrysler engineers were engaged in developing a V-16 aircraft engine and a V-12 tank engine, both of which had hemispherical combustion chambers. Although neither of these engines reached production status due to the war's end, their performance and efficiency were excellent, impressing the engineers involved.

With some known advantages of a hemispherical combustion chamber, why hadn't it achieved more widespread use in automobiles? There were two basic reasons, Chrysler found. The Hemi head had a reputation for roughness and proclivity for high-octane fuels. Also, the inherent complexity and cost didn't lend itself to mass production. However, Chrysler Corporation had years of experience building relatively high-compression engines. In 1924, Chrysler introduced high compression in its namesake line of cars. Four years later, it turned the automotive world on its ear with the 1928 Red Head engine with an unheard-of 6.2:1 compression ratio.

The Chrysler engineering team was up to the task of developing a truly revolutionary passenger-car engine. James C. Zeder was director of Engineering and Research. He was the younger brother of Fred Zeder, who, along with Carl Breer and O. R. Skelton, left Studebaker in 1920 at the behest of Walter P. Chrysler to establish the Chrysler Corporation. Working under James Zeder was Ray White, in charge of experimental design; William E. Drinkard, head of laboratory research and development;

and Mel Carpentier, in charge of production engine design. These men relished the challenge of working the bugs—real or imagined—out of the Hemi head and making it viable for mass-produced automobiles.

Chrysler began testing a great many passenger-car engines from both domestic and foreign auto makers. Ev Moeller witnessed these engines being tested. He started with Chrysler in 1939 and graduated from the Chrysler Institute in 1941. He was assigned to the aircraft engine program during the war, and in 1947, he was moved to the Engine Development Laboratory.

"We tested every engine in site," Moeller says. "One of the engines that we worked on was the Healey, which was an English small passenger-car engine that had a pushrod-operated overhead valvetrain. It had two camshafts, one on each side of the block. The pushrods came up to operate the overhead valves. It was a long-stroke, Hemi configuration and the thing that was surprising was it was the highest powered and most efficient engine we had ever tested."

Lab testing of the single-cylinder engine with the four different head designs was supervised by John Platner, who had joined Chrysler in 1931 as a member of the first class of the Chrysler Institute of Engineering Graduate School. Platner worked in Engine Development his entire career with the company, and made his presence felt over the years.

What they found was contrary to what had been doctrine concerning the Hemi head: this cylinder head actually displayed knock-limiting characteristics. To achieve the thermal efficiency of the Hemi head at 7.0:1, the L-head required a compression ratio of 10.0:1 at 1200 rpm, 9.4:1 at 2000 rpm, 8.9:1 at 2800 rpm and 8.5:1 at 3600 rpm. The F-head performed much like the L-head. The overhead-valve head was somewhat better than these two, but it suffered losses of volumetric efficiency and valve durability.

The Hemi head was a superior performer in all respects. With the intake valve closest to the intake manifold and the exhaust valve directly across from it on the other side of the hemispherical chamber with an included valve angle of 58½ deg., the fuel-air mixture entered, burned and exited efficiently. The Hemi-

This V–8 Hemi-head prototype engine shows how the spark-plug wires were originally grouped on the valve covers. The left-hand exhaust pipe passed underneath the oil pan to join the right-hand exhaust pipe for a single exhaust system. Chrysler

The Chrysler FirePower 331 ci V–8 was introduced in 1951. The engine shown on this display stand featured chrome-plated parts for show. The spark-plug wires were hidden by the small cover on top of the valve cover. Chrysler

The Chrysler FirePower V–8 was standard equipment in such cars as the Chrysler New Yorker. Chrysler

head design also extended valve life and promoted sealing by aiding effective uniform cooling of the valve seats. The engineers found the stability of the valve seats in the Hemi head to be excellent.

With these encouraging results, Zeder's team decided it was time to test the Hemi head on one of its engines. A standard Chrysler straight-six engine was selected and a special double-overhead-camshaft head with hemispherical combustion chambers was designed and built. Bench tests showed a significant performance gain over the standard six-cylinder engine. The engine, with the designation A161, was installed in a Chrysler to test real-world conditions by Wallace E. Zierer, who was in charge of automobile testing. The car

ran effortlessly on the then-standard eighty-octane regular gas. Roughness, which had been a theoretical concern, was absent, thus affirming the use of a Hemi head in a passenger car. It was a research and development milestone for Chrysler.

From a production standpoint, however, the chain-driven double-over-head-valve design was complex and expensive, and serviceability would be a problem. A simpler, less costly valvetrain design had to be worked out. What the team developed was a pushrod-actuated Hemi-head straight-six with a greatly simplified valvetrain at less expense.

Birth of the FirePower

Despite the successful test results, a Chrysler Hemi engine, or even a Hemi

V–8 for that matter, was by no means certain. Convincing Chrysler upper management was a formidable task, because there were detractors within management, as well as the engineering staff itself, of both the Hemi head and the proposed V–8 configuration.

Drinkard, who joined Chrysler in 1934 and became manager of the Engine Development Laboratory in 1943, remembers the battles in the boardrooms of Chrysler over this new engine. "There were just two guys, as far as I'm concerned, that believed in the idea of the Hemi V–8 engine and tried to sell it," Drinkard recalls vividly. "Those two guys were John Platner and myself. There wasn't anybody else. Anytime you work in a big corporation, if you've got some idea and try to sell it, look out for all those guys who are going to sell something else and belittle you. That is exactly what happened. Fred Zeder said, 'Look fellas, I'm not going to have any part of a V–8 engine. We've made our money on a straight eight and that's all we're going to have.' We had all these research guys in there trying to confuse the waters. Finally, K. T. Keller, the chief operating officer, said, 'Bill, I think maybe you've got the right plan.' That was the thing that turned the whole thing around." Drinkard later co-authored a paper with Mel Carpentier published by the Society of Automotive Engineers (SAE) in July 1951 detailing the laboratory findings.

Prior to and just after the war, Chrysler had tested a number of engine configurations with a multiplicity of intake manifold designs, intake and exhaust valve juxtaposition, and other mechanical variations. These included one inline five-cylinder engine, several inline six-cylinder engines, one 90 deg. V–6, and several 60 deg. V–6s and 90 deg. V–8s. One experimental V–6, the A93, had both overhead and underhead valves. The overhead intake valves were push-rod actuated while the underhead exhaust valves were directly actuated by the camshaft tappets. No concept was beyond consideration in Chrysler's search for increased engine performance. The 90 deg. V–6 was found to be unsatisfactory for smoothness, and the length and weight of a straight-eight were no longer thought to be acceptable. The compact V–8 engine appeared to be the standard for the future. Cadillac and Oldsmobile were working on V–8 engine designs for introduction in 1949, so it was this configuration Zeder and his fellow engineers selected for use with the Hemi head.

By 1948, Chrysler had a 330 ci Hemi-head V–8 undergoing testing, the A182 designed by Ray White's department. The A182 prototype Hemi V–8 was run extensively on the dynamometer to evaluate its performance after optimizing variables like camshaft timing, fuel mixture and ignition timing. It was then evaluated in a road-test Chrysler car with satisfactory results. Chrysler management was sufficiently impressed with the results of all of the A182 engines tested that approval was given for an engine of this type and size to be designed for production.

Mel Carpentier's department then designed the A239 engine, which became the first production Hemi V–8, later christened the Chrysler FirePower. It had a slightly larger displacement of 331 ci. The resulting design was shorter and lighter than the A182, and was designed with manufacturing considerations in mind.

Robert Cahill joined Chrysler in 1936. He started working in the engine development lab in 1938 and stayed there until 1953. He witnessed the first-generation Hemi's development first-hand within the tough parameters established by Drinkard. Cahill recalls, "Drinkard laid down the spec that he wanted us to be able to pass a thousand hour test on a certain schedule we had. He wanted the engine to be able to run 100,000 miles without having to replace major parts. He wanted the bearings, valves, pistons and rings to last 100,000 miles. There was a lot of effort made to do that."

One of the most worrisome problems was in the area of camshaft wear. Bert Bouwkamp knew firsthand the difficulties encountered in making this key engine component last the requisite number of miles. He entered the Chrysler Institute in February 1949, graduating in June 1951. Starting work in the Engine Laboratory, he coordinated development of the 241 ci Dodge Red Ram Hemi. He remained in the lab for one year, then moved on to the DeSoto engine plant to supervise production of the DeSoto FireDome V–8, where he was assistant motor engineer.

"This was our first overhead valve engine," Bouwkamp says, "and the biggest problem with the Hemi was camshaft wear. We didn't have experience with valvetrain loads, and we ran into severe wear between the camshaft and the face of the tappet. Some engines failed in a few thousand miles. We had some failures right within the engine plant and after tearing them down, [it was clear] they wouldn't have gone 100 miles."

Bob Rodger was head of the group assigned to solve this accelerated wear problem. It became apparent the problem had to be attacked on a number of different levels.

"To solve this," Bouwkamp continues, "it took a change in the material of the tappet to chilled cast iron, a change to the spherical radius of the tappet to try to reduce the unit loading,

a graphite-based anti-scuff coating, and an additive in the oil to finally solve the problem."

Fred Shrimpton was truly unique among all the designers, engineers and drafters who have worked at Chrysler. His career there spans more than six decades and he has been able to observe virtually every major engine design in that time. He recalls the first day he applied for work at Chrysler in 1929 as if it were yesterday. The current six-story building at Oakland Avenue in Highland Park was only three stories then. He started work as a tracer and had risen to chief layout man when interest in the Hemi V–8 and the prospect of its production finally crystallized.

"Mel Carpentier came up to me one day," Shrimpton remembers, "and said, 'I want you to lay out a Hemi head.' I laid out all three engines—the Chrysler, the Dodge and the DeSoto. That was a lot of fun. I really liked it. It was something different. Then we had a strike, so I rolled all the stuff up. We were gone for 104 days; it was a long strike. When I came back, those drawings were gone, but we had already started on detailing drawings. In fact, we knew so little about them, we made details right off the layout drawings. The big problem was getting spark plugs down through the center and how to seal them."

Because the spark plug was located between the intake and exhaust valves and slightly offset from the cylinder's centerline, some means had to be developed to permit changing the plugs without having to remove the large valve covers. A steel tube was designed with a flange at the lower end that acted as a gasket as the spark plug was screwed into the cylinder head. Snapping the spark-plug wire onto the spark plug was facilitated by a long ceramic boot. To prevent oil from leaking between the tube and the valve cover, an ignition wire cover, or channel, compressed a neoprene O-ring with a steel washer, creating a seal around each tube as the ignition wire cover was screwed into place. The ignition wires were hidden by the ignition wire cover until they exited the back of the valve cover near the distributor, giving this first-generation Hemi engine a clean look.

Chrysler's new engine featured other improvements. The crankshaft employed shot-peened and machined undercut fillets to eliminate tool marks

Chrysler Division president Ed Quinn, left, and James C. Zeder, vice-president of engineering, pose with the A311 Indianapolis 500 racing engine. Chrysler was forced to reduce displacement from stock to meet the rules, cutting the engine's power. Chrysler

For the 1951 model year, Chrysler introduced the Chrysler FirePower V–8. The engine had a displacement of 331.1 ci and produced 180 hp at 4000 rpm and 312 lb-ft of torque at 2000 rpm. This represented a more than forty percent boost in horsepower and a sixteen percent increase in torque over the straight-eight engine of 1950. And it was 9½ in. shorter than the inline engine.

The Chrysler FirePower V–8 was introduced in the long-running (since 1939) Chrysler Saratoga and New Yorker, as well as the Chrysler Imperial and Crown Imperial. The Imperial was the flagship of Chrysler; the Chrysler Imperial 80 had been introduced in 1926. The engine was a marketer's and advertiser's delight. While not a high-performance engine per se, it was Chrysler's first V–8 passenger-car engine and it bristled with features that made great advertising copy. It developed more power than either the Cadillac or Oldsmobile V–8s, and didn't require premium-grade fuel like its competitors.

Harold Welch began working at Chrysler in 1935. As did all graduate engineers, he entered the Chrysler Institute, a two-year work-study program. In 1937 he was assigned to the mechanical laboratory. In 1940, he moved to the engine development laboratory and became assistant manager, under William Drinkard. He recalls the impact the new Chrysler FirePower had on the automotive industry.

"It was jokingly said," he says today, "it made the lights on the top floor of the General Motors building burn extra hours at night. It's sometimes blamed for kicking off what was generally referred to as the horsepower race."

As planned, Chrysler expanded availability of the Hemi-head design to other makes. In 1952, the DeSoto Fire-Dome V–8 made its debut with a displacement of 276 ci with 160 hp at 4400 rpm. Dodge received its Red Ram Hemi V–8 in 1953. It was the smallest of all the Chrysler Hemi V–8s, with a displacement of 241.3 ci; it generated 140 hp at 4400 rpm and 220 lb-ft of torque at 2000 rpm. The engine was offered in the 114 and 119 in. wheelbase versions of the V–8-equipped Coronet that year.

High-Performance Development

The Chrysler Hemi-head V–8 had untapped reserves of power, and the engineers knew it. The research, design

and surface roughness and greatly improve fatigue strength. The use of hydraulic tappets was to achieve quiet valve operation and to enhance the life through constant control of opening and closing ramps.

Chrysler worked with Carter to design a water-jacketed carburetor throttle-valve body with integral automatic choke to prevent engine stalling due to carburetor icing. A dual-breaker distributor provided a reserve of ignition voltage at high speeds.

The durability of this new Chrysler engine—given the name FirePower—was as important as all the engineering that went into it. More than 8,000 hours of dynamometer testing and more than 500,000 miles on test cars were involved in ensuring long-term durability. The engine was finally ready and released for production.

and development of the engine had been slow and deliberate. Increasing performance was, indeed, the engineers' goal, but high performance was not—at first.

In a paper presented to the SAE at the National Passenger Car, Body and Materials Meeting in Detroit in March 1952, Zeder recalled how further development—high-performance development—came about.

Zeder wrote: "Then we met the 'hotrod' boys—or rather they adopted us with all the gusto attending induction into any other tribe of wild Indians. We, who live within the industry, have learned to accept without too much resistance the utilitarian place which our product holds in the scheme of things; but it was a pleasure and, in many ways, an inspiration to meet a group of men in whom are rekindled the enthusiams [sic] of an earlier era; men to who owning and driving a car are sport and adventure, and not merely a chore inherited by default from the streetcar motorman."

Zeder and his team were just as intrigued as the "hotrod boys" in learning what the maximum performance potential of the engine was, even if there wasn't a real-world application for it. Once again, two key areas were explored: compression ratio and volumetric efficiency. A production Chrysler FirePower was fitted with pistons, giving compression ratios of 7.5:1, 10.0:1 and 12.5:1. The rest of the engine remained stock. The engineers achieved a fifteen percent boost in power with 12.5:1 pistons over the 7.5:1 pistons. However, the engine required the equivalent octane rating of 130 performance number. Running double-digit compression ratios would have to wait for the advent of superior-grade gasoline.

The most dramatic gains in power would come from attacking the engine's volumetric efficiency. To establish a realistic baseline from which to work, it was decided to discard the stock exhaust manifolds for the streamlined, steel-tube exhaust type. This alone produced an 18 lb-ft increase in torque and a further 13 hp. The other three areas affecting volumetric efficiency were valve ports, intake manifolding and carburetion, and camshafts.

While the Hemi head permitted larger intake and exhaust valves, there was room to make them even larger. The

One of the high-performance Chrysler FirePower derivatives Zeder and his team developed was the K–310. It featured four carburetors, log-type intake manifold and streamlined exhaust manifold. Chrysler

intake valve was increased 0.125 in. and the exhaust valve by 0.25 in. The ports were increased to match the increase in flow.

Chrysler engineers decided on two approaches regarding intake manifolding and carburetion. For mid-range, or high torque, they designed a manifold to accept four inline single-barrel carburetors, each one feeding two cylinders. For high speed, or high power, the four carburetors sat atop a simple runner manifold, similar to racing designs of the day.

The standard FirePower engine used a camshaft giving 252 deg. intake duration, 244 deg. exhaust duration, with 30 deg. of overlap. Three special camshafts were developed for the test engine. The first was a 260/260 deg. design with 40 deg. of overlap. The second was 270/260 deg. with 50 deg. of

Introduced in 1952, the DeSoto FireDome V–8 had a displacement of 276 ci and was rated at 160 hp. Chrysler

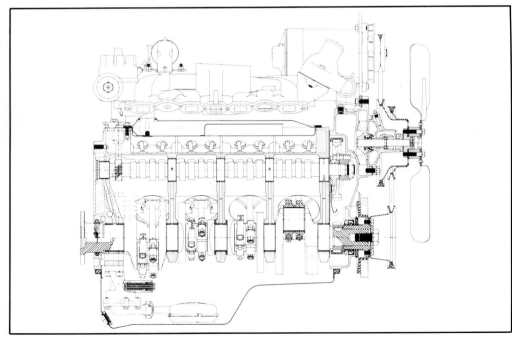

This assembly layout drawing of the DeSoto FireDome V–8 displayed the draftman's art, now lost in the age of computer-aided design. Chrysler

overlap, and the most radical design was 280/270 deg. with 60 deg. of overlap. Lift was increased with all three camshafts. "This is one of the earliest places the electronic computer was used to design the camshaft," Welch states. "The computer came along just in time to develop a new mathematical formula that permitted better cam design with minimum stress and maximum performance."

Test results surprised no one. The Hemi responded exceedingly well to these modifications. With the high-flow heads and high-torque intake manifold, the engine gained 42 hp with a 30 lb-ft boost in torque. The three camshafts were tested in this engine with the 270/260/50 cam giving the best all-around performance increase. The total increase in the Hemi's output over the new baseline engine was 60 lb-ft of torque and 95 hp.

The high-torque induction was replaced by the high-speed carburetor-manifold setup, and the tests were run again with all three camshafts. The 280/270/60 camshaft produced the best results throughout the rpm range. Corrected brake horsepower was 308.6 with 341.7 lb-ft of torque—with stock pistons! To see what a boost in compression ratio could do, the 12.6:1 pistons were installed. All previous runs were made using premium-grade gasoline; for this run they ran the equivalent of iso-octane plus 1.0 cc of lead to prevent knock. Torque increased to 385 lb-ft with 353 hp—all this from a 331 ci engine.

In typical engineering understatement, James Zeder wrote, "the basic FirePower cylinder gives performance comparable with Indianapolis engines, which have been developed for power without regard to any other purpose." In his concluding remarks, Zeder was more enthusiastic, stating, "we remain unalterably convinced that, in the battle of the combustion chambers, the spherical segment chamber has demonstrated unquestioned supremacy."

Production Performance Increases

In 1954, the first wave of increased power appeared. The Chrysler Fire-Power now developed 195 hp at 4400 rpm, still at a 7.5:1 compression ratio, but a new four-barrel-carburetor version developed 235 hp. The Dodge Red Ram was offered in a 7.1:1 compression ratio developing 140 hp at 4400 rpm, and a 7.5:1 version with 150 hp. The DeSoto

FireDome now produced 170 hp at 4400 rpm.

Chrysler Corporation was poised to throw off its conservative image. The high-performance development work that showed the Hemi's potential was about to bear fruit that would attract the attention of the entire automotive world, and it was decided that this new car would be introduced for 1955. The car was the Chrysler 300.

Bob Rodger joined Chrysler in 1939 and entered the Chrysler Institute. After graduating, he was assigned to the Engine Development Lab in 1941. He was a key man on Drinkard's team in the development of outstanding durability for the A239 FirePower engine. By 1954, he was resident chief engineer of the Chrysler car division. He knew well the performance potential of the FirePower engine and proposed the concept of a high-powered model with good handling and unique styling. This early product planning proposal resulted in the 1955 Chrysler 300.

From the time it began rolling off the assembly line in January 1955, it became *the* car to road test by automotive journalists. The 300's performance left them agog, establishing a high-water mark in acceleration, handling and top speed. The 331 ci FirePower now had a compression ratio of 8.5:1, a 280/270/60 mechanical camshaft, and two Carter four-barrel carburetors. It developed 300 hp—hence the car's designation—at 5200 rpm and 345 lb-ft of torque at 3200 rpm. The only other car that even came close was the Cadillac Eldorado with 270 hp, but it weighed nearly half a ton more than the 4,000 lb. Chrysler 300.

A less-potent 331 FirePower was offered in the Chrysler New Yorker Deluxe and the Imperial, having 250 hp at 4600 rpm and 340 lb-ft of torque at 2800 rpm. To round out the Chrysler FirePower line-up, a new smaller-displacement V–8 with 301 ci was offered in the Chrysler Windsor Deluxe with an 8.0:1 compression ratio, developing 188 hp at 4400 rpm and 275 lb-ft of torque at 2400 rpm.

Over at Dodge, the Red Ram Hemi received an increase in displacement to 270 ci, boosting output to 175 hp. This new, larger mill was standard in the Coronet and Royal. The Custom Royal had slightly more power—8 hp to be exact. An optional engine was available in all three models. The Custom Royal

Dodge introduced its Hemi, the Red Ram V–8, in 1953. Its displacement was just over 241 ci and was rated at 140 hp. Plymouth was the only division not to offer a Hemi V–8 of its own. Chrysler

engine could be ordered with a Special Equipment Power Package that used a four-barrel carburetor. This produced 193 hp at 4400 rpm with 245 lb-ft of torque at 2800 rpm.

For 1955, the DeSoto FireDome also was increased in displacement, to 291 ci. With a two-barrel carburetor, it was rated at 185 hp. A four-barrel version, called the Fireflight, was offered which developed 200 hp.

Racing Success

Until the advent of the Chrysler 300 in 1955, Chryslers were not the car of choice for circle-track and endurance races. During the early fifties, however, Briggs Cunningham was the most visible privateer who believed in the Chrysler Hemi V–8 and campaigned his cars, most

visibly at LeMans. Cunningham had raced various automotive concoctions during the forties. In 1950, his team won tenth and eleventh places overall at Le Mans in mildly modified Cadillacs.

Cunningham's first attempt with the Hemi at Le Mans was in 1951, after founding the B. S. Cunningham Company with partners Bill Frick and Phil Walters in West Palm Beach, Florida. Chrysler was willing to help as much as it could, and the high-performance development work on the FirePower found its way into his C Series race cars. The cars were uniquely Cunningham, using an American V–8 engine in a chassis of his company's own design, as was the body. The striking blue-and-white C–2s that hit Le Mans were heavy but they were fast—152 mph down the long

The Chrysler 300 quickly became a legend on the racetracks around the country, lending credence to the words "stock car." It was one of the most desirable cars of the fifties to own and drive—a true gentleman's express. The combination of two four-barrel carburetors, a stiff mechanical camshaft and the hemispherical-combustion-chamber cylinder heads produced 300 hp from the 331 ci FirePower V–8. No other American-made car at the time could match its performance. David Gooley

Mulsanne straight. The following year the sanctioning body of Le Mans issued a new requirement, stating a manufacturer had to build a minimum of twenty-five cars in order to race as a production car. Cunningham built exactly twenty-five C3 and C4 roadsters and coupes combined to qualify.

In the 1952 Le Mans race, Cunningham drove twenty of the twenty-four hours and finished in fourth place, all the more remarkable since he was in

his forties. Team Cunningham also raced the cars in America over the next several years as well, before closing his company in 1955.

On the NASCAR circuit, Oldsmobile and Hudson seesawed for dominance during the early fifties. That all changed in 1955. The Bob Rodger-conceived Chrysler 300 won twenty-seven of the forty-five races that year, winning the Grand National title.

Back in the fifties, there was room for a full-size spare tire—wire wheels, huge whitewalls and all. The small fins on the car would grow to amazing proportions in a few years. David Gooley

Factory racing of the Hemi might have taken other forms if the A311 engine program had reached fruition. Harold Welch remembers how Chrysler almost went racing at Indianapolis. "This engine," he says, "was first used to test tires for Firestone, then Goodyear. The A311 was made with large ports and roller tappets. John Platner and Don Moore were deeply involved with the project. They used a Hilborn fuel-injection system, which was common at Indianapolis at that time. That car was used

for many miles of high-speed testing and it was able to easily run at regular Indianapolis speeds.

"As part of the dedication of the Chrysler Proving Grounds in June of 1954," Welch continues, "the first four finishing drivers of that year's Indianapolis 500 mile race were invited to bring their winning cars to try them on the new highly banked 4.7 mile oval track. All of the drivers held their cars wide open through the turns, which was the first time any of them had had an opportunity to do so. Jack McGrath was the fastest, with an amazing 179 miles per hour. Even more amazing was that the Chrysler-powered Kurtis Kraft tire-test car then ran 182 miles per hour!

"It showed this Hemi with its pushrod valvegear could definitely compete very nicely with the Offys. The rules at

Indianapolis permitted stock-block engines to have that much displacement, but then they changed the rules to 272 cubic inches. We shortened the stroke to get 272 cubic inches, and that's how they entered the race the next year, but didn't quite make it. It's interesting that at 331 cubic inches, it was so successful they changed the rules."

It wouldn't be the last time a sanctioning body would change the rules again because of the Chrysler Hemi's inherent performance superiority.

Production-Car Improvements

There were changes in the Hemi-engine line-up for 1956. At Chrysler, the 301 ci Hemi was dropped and a new 354 ci Hemi was introduced. The displacement increase was achieved by increasing the bore from 3.81 to 3.92 in. while

23

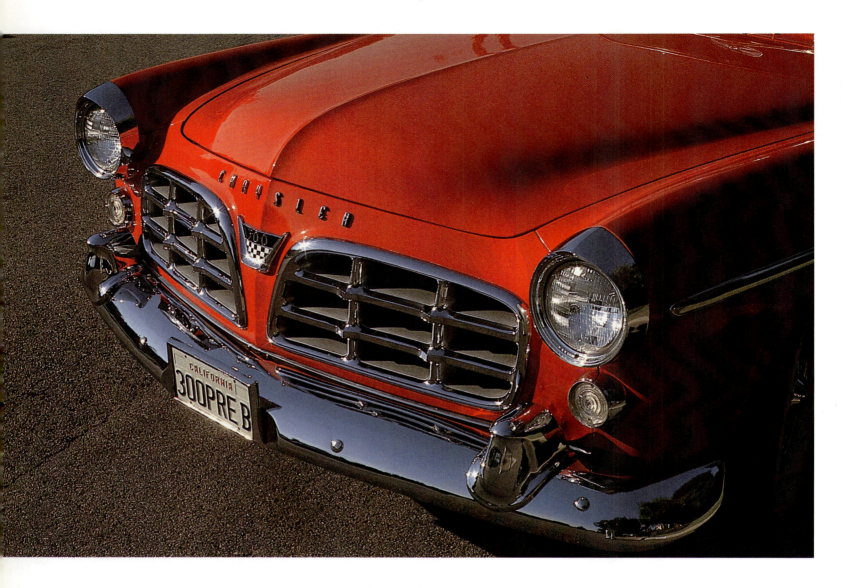

The Chrysler 300 had its own distinctive escutcheon mounted between the grille openings. And it had the horsepower to match the numbers. The car blazed a trail of wins on the NASCAR circuit that lent status to the version in Chrysler showrooms. David Gooley

Previous page
The Chrysler 300 of 1955 was a traffic-stopper. There were more expensive cars on the road, but none was faster. It ushered in a new era of large fast cars, soon to be known as muscle cars. David Gooley

keeping the 3.63 in. stroke. The 354 Hemi had a 9.0:1 compression ratio and produced 280 hp at 4600 rpm, with 380 lb-ft of torque at 2800 rpm. This engine

was standard in the New Yorker, New Yorker Newport and New Yorker St. Regis. This was the last year for the Chrysler 331 ci Hemi in the Windsor line, which was now offered in a 225 hp version, or the optional 250 hp powerplant. Chrysler's performance flagship, the 300, now took on its famous letter designation sequence. The 300 B was powered by a 340 hp 354 Hemi, churning out 385 lb-ft of torque at 3400 rpm. The optional 10.0:1 compression engine developed 355 hp at 5200 rpm, and 405 lb-ft of torque at 3400 rpm.

The Chrysler 300 really did have a mystique about it. With its now-legendary racing victories and awesome horsepower, the 300 B turned heads whenever one drove by. The legend grew in 1956, with Chrysler again taking

the NASCAR title. The colorful Carl Kiekhaefer-sponsored team won sixteen races in a row. Chrysler capitalized on the success of its 300 in its advertising. In an ad picturing a 300 B getting the checkered flag under the bright lights of a nighttime race, the copy read, "Let's get one thing straight . . . Chrysler has won every major competition in 1956! And don't confuse Chrysler's Grand Slam wins in all the big events with those 'in their class' wins that you may have read about. When Chrysler competes it competes against all comers!"

Almost lost in the hoopla over the 300 B were improvements in the Dodge and DeSoto Hemis for 1956. Dodge introduced a raised-block (RB or raised-B) Hemi with 315 ci, having a bore and stroke of 3.63x3.60 in. It developed 218 hp in standard trim for use in the Custom

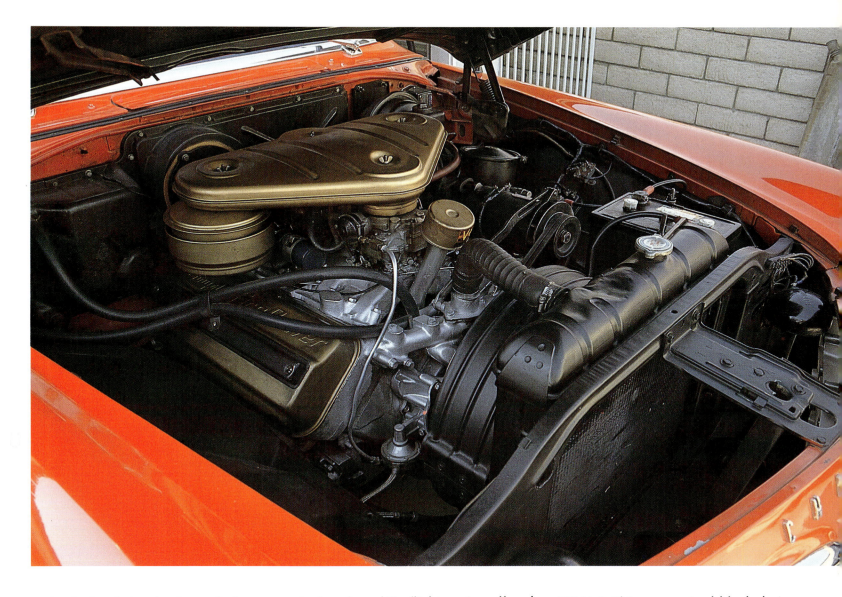

and Custom Royal. There were two optional 315 ci Hemis, one developing 230 hp and the other 260 hp. The small 270 ci Hemi was still standard in the Coronet, now rated at 189 hp. The 354 ci Hemi was optional in the Coronet; with a 10.0:1 compression ratio, it pumped out 340 hp at 5200 rpm and 380 lb-ft of torque at 3800 rpm.

DeSoto also received a raised-block Hemi in 1956. This new two-barrel, 330 ci FireDome V-8 developed 230 hp, but the four-barrel Fireflight version offered 255 hp. DeSoto buyers demanding maximum power ordered the dual four-barrel 341.1 ci Adventurer with 320 hp. The DeSoto received a boost in its lagging image when it was selected as pace car for the 1956 Indy 500.

All of Chrysler Corporation's car divisions received all-new sheet metal for 1957, and the Fin Era was now in full swing. Chrysler reduced its offerings from seven distinct models to four: Windsor, Saratoga (absent since 1953), New Yorker and the 300 C. Horsepower kept climbing, as did compression ratios. The venerable 331 Hemi was dropped. The Windsor was now powered by a 285 hp 354 ci Hemi, running a 9.25:1 compression ratio. The Saratoga had 10 hp more. Now, there was a new Hemi: the 392 V-8. This was a raised-block design with a bore and stroke of 4.00x3.90 in. With the new increase in displacement came larger valves: intake valves were 2.0 in. and exhaust valves 1.75 in. This increased displacement and breathing, of course, brought increased power: 325 hp at 4600 rpm with 430 lb-ft of torque at 2800 rpm. The New Yorker came standard with this engine.

The most powerful Chrysler 392 Hemi that year was reserved for the 300 C. The dual four-barrel, radically cammed 392 Hemi with 9.25:1 compression developed 375 hp at 5200 rpm, with 420 lb-ft of torque at 4000 rpm. The optional 10.0:1 compression 392 was rated at 390 hp, with 10 lb-ft more torque at slightly higher rpm. Some wondered just where this horsepower would end,

27

but in truth it had already begun to level off.

The Chrysler Imperial also received its annual horsepower boost. The 280 hp 354 Hemi of the previous year was replaced by a 325 hp 392 for 1957. There was no optional engine for the three Imperial models, and really, in a luxury car like this, one didn't need it.

The Dodge line of models was expanded and now included the six- and eight-cylinder Coronet, Coronet Custom, Royal, Custom Royal, Suburban, Sierra and Custom Sierra. The standard V–8 in the Coronet, Royal, Custom Royal and Suburban was the 315 bored out to 325 ci. Power was now 245 hp with 320 lb-ft of torque. There were three optional V–8 engines for the Coronet: the 285 or 310 hp 325 with 9.25:1 compression, or the top-of-the-line 340 hp 354 from the previous year. Optional in the Royal and Custom Royal were the 285 and 310 hp 325s. If you ordered the optional 285 hp 325 for your Suburban, it became the Sierra; if you opted for the 310 hp version, it became the Custom Sierra.

Some automotive pundits felt the late 1950s were the era of excess. This was evident in model names as well as aesthetics. DeSoto was a prime example. For 1957, you could choose from the Firesweep, FireDome, Fireflight and Adventurer. For less fanciful types, there was also the Explorer and Shopper station wagons. This was to be the last year for the Hemi engine in DeSotos. There was the two-barrel FireDome 341 ci engine with 270 hp, the four-barrel 341 ci Fireflight with 295 hp, and the dual four-barrel 345 ci engine offered in the Adventurer with 345 hp. The Hemi would be replaced the following year by the Turboflash V–8. All this fire and flash was to no avail, however, as DeSoto ceased car production with its 1961 line.

The days for the Chrysler Corporation Hemi were indeed numbered. The company had been working on a less-expensive Wedge-head design, and engines with the new cylinder head made

The Hemi V–8 version used in the DeSoto was called the FireDome. Note the absence of spark-plug wires; they were hidden under the DeSoto FireDome Eight wire cover on the valve cover. Musclecar Review

their debut in 1958. At Dodge, the lone Hemi offering was the 325, which was at a distinct disadvantage when stacked up against the new 350 and 361 ci Wedge engines that developed more horsepower.

The situation was somewhat better at Chrysler, where the Hemi still dominated the engine line-up. The Windsor came equipped with the 290 hp 354, the Saratoga with the 310 hp 354 and the New Yorker with the 345 hp 392. The new 300 D came with a 380 hp 392; the optional 392 with fuel injection was rated at 390 hp. All Chrysler Hemi engines this year packed a 10.0:1 compression ratio. The Imperial models came with the same engine as the New

Yorker. According to Chrysler Corporation literature, this was the last year of production for the first-generation Hemi engine in Chrysler, Dodge and Imperial.

Why was such a thoroughly proven engine scrapped? Drinkard will be the first to state the Hemi was replaced for purely economic reasons. Welch agrees, but says there were other reasons involved as well.

"To our chagrin," he says, "our management thought we were spending more producing our engine than Ford and General Motors were with their wedge-shaped combustion chambers, and manufacturing was interested in building a new, central engine plant to build engines [for all divisions]. So, for primarily economic reasons, the B and raised-B engines built at Trention eventually replaced the Hemi. They were somewhat lighter than the Hemi and more economical as far as material is concerned, and then, of course, the cars began to get heavier, so that the V–8 for the Dodge and DeSoto ended up being too small. That combination of things replaced the first generation family of Hemis with the B and raised-B."

The Ramchargers

The Hemi was gone but not forgotten by some at Chrysler. Around 1958, a small group of Chrysler engineers formed a club to share their interest in cars in general and high-performance cars in particular. Tom Hoover was one of the men in this group. Having received his masters degree in physics in 1955, he entered Chrysler through the Chrysler Institute and in 1957, went to work in the area of fuel injection. He got to know like-minded engineers over the next year, and what first started out as casual gatherings eventually evolved into one of the most aggressive drag-racing teams in the United States.

"In the cafeteria in Engineering at

32

lunchtime," Hoover recalls, "a number of us who had performance vehicles, which was rather rare in those days among the Chrysler cars, would get together. There were six or eight [of us] initially. Wayne Erikson and myself were the two primary instigators. The idea was to have just a group so that we could go to the drag races together, cooperate and help one another out."

This group called themselves the Ramchargers. At night, they would demoralize other drag racers on North Woodward Avenue in Detroit and on weekends, set records at Detroit Dragway. These engineers had access to the research and development work that had been done on the Hemi and they applied it to their personal cars. Then they concocted a plan to build an altered vehicle for the B/Altered class in sanctioned drag racing, and the *High and Mighty* started to take shape. The car they used was a 1949 Plymouth Business Coupe, and it was extensively modified in the home garage of Jack McPhearson, one of the Ramchargers.

"Dan Mancini and I built the engine," Hoover says. "Gale Porter over at Dodge got for us a 354 Hemi truck engine that had dropped an exhaust valve. It became the engine for the *High and Mighty*. It was a joke with us at the time because we had roughly $200 invested in it. We bought a new set of Jahns pistons. Jim Hider had a place over near the Detroit Airport. We came up with a camshaft profile and ol' Jim would do it for a reasonable price. Jeff Baker at Chrysler designed the plenum-ram manifold, and we used reinforced radiator hose for the trumpets. The *High and Mighty* was the grandaddy of the tunnel-ram manifold."

Getting all this new-found horsepower to the ground was a problem due to the limitations of tires in the late fifties. Troy Simonsen joined Chrysler in 1958 and the Ramchargers shortly thereafter. He relates how they solved the problem of traction.

"With the *High and Mighty,* we sat down and thought about the vehicle dynamics of drag racing. The problem was getting all the traction you can. We wanted the car high, to get weight shift. We had a unique suspension that was intended to transfer the weight equally to both the rear wheels so that the torque of the driveshaft and the tendency to lift the right wheel was offset.

That car," Simonsen remembers, "was tall enough that you could crawl under it on your hands and knees, almost."

This impromptu club grew from its rather inauspicious beginnings over the years to race the Max Wedge and 426 Hemi engines, and the Ramchargers became one of the biggest draws in sanctioned drag racing. More importantly, the Ramchargers had a dramatic impact on Chrysler Corporation's racing engine development. The company's racing success and attendant public image were a direct result of the enthusiastic efforts of these engineers. Some of the others who joined the Ramchargers included Dick Maxwell, Dan Knapp, Tom Coddington, Jerry Donley, Herm Moser, Jim Thornton, Mike Buckle and Gary Congdon.

"I doubt that there would have been a drag-racing program without the Ramchargers," Hoover says. "I really believe if the company had made an attempt to do drag racing as they did, I doubt they would have been successful at all if the Ramchargers cornerstone had not been available."

The ability of the hemispherical-combustion-chamber cylinder head to make power would prove itself again when the new Wedge-head engines showed their limitations on the high-banked ovals of NASCAR racing around the country. The Hemi was momentarily eclipsed by the Wedge head until it became clear that something more—much more—was needed.

426 Race Hemi
In the Winner's Circle 1964–1970

Larry Adams, who was in charge of race-engine development, came into my office, just sat down in the chair and said, "Bill, that engine isn't going to last. We aren't going to finish the race."

Willem L. Weertman

As the first-generation Hemi faded from the scene, the Wedge-head engines took over the dynamometer labs and engine bays. In 1957, the 318 ci Wedge was introduced in the Plymouth Fury. The 350 and 361 ci Wedge engines were released in the Dodge line in 1958; Plymouth got the 350 ci Wedge the same year. The 383 and 413 Wedges in Chryslers came out the following year. The Imperial was now powered by a 413 Wedge, not the Hemi.

Interestingly, the 1959 Chrysler 300 E, now powered by the Golden Lion 413 Wedge, produced no more power than the 392 Hemi of the previous year. Some automotive writers thought this a moot point. Horsepower was horsepower, after all. One test pegged the 380 hp 300 E at 17.2 sec. for the quarter mile doing 92 mph through the lights.

The Wedge V–8 continued its evolution into the new decade. In truth, the new Wedge engines were more than adequate in the street cars that Chrysler built. The Max Wedge 413 and 426 high-performance racing engines proved their capabilities on drag strips around the country, whether they were campaigned by the Ramchargers (and Plymouth's rival Golden Commandos) or the big and small names in drag racing. Circle-track racing—NASCAR—was another matter.

In 1964, Mopar and its new Hemi swept the Daytona 500, and in 1969, Dodge built its Daytona and named it in honor of the race, above. Left, the drag-race Hemi engine on this Dick Landy Dodge 330 was fitted with chrome valve covers. The block and intake manifold were painted Hemi Orange. Michael Dregni; David Gooley

Chrysler cars, specifically Dodge and Plymouth, were not frequently in the stock-car winner's circle. A resolution passed by the Automobile Manufacturers Association (AMA) on June 6, 1957, banned car manufacturers from openly supporting racing wins as a reflection of their street car's performance. The AMA felt such practices encouraged reckless driving. The manufacturers went along with the resolution, fearing that failure to do so would result in unfavorable legislation from Washington. The car makers were forced to sell the racing cars and parts, usually to those teams they sponsored, and back off. The AMA did not clamp down on the production of high-performance street cars, however. NASCAR did not view the AMA ban as a threat, because it once again permitted the little guy to have a fighting chance for the winner's circle.

What the resolution succeeded in doing was force the handful of car makers active before the ban to become creative in their means of researching, developing and distributing racing hardware. This was achieved in part by the NASCAR rules that took shape stating that if a given make, model and engine was to be raced, it had to be a production vehicle or option. This had more or

The Chrysler 426 Hemi was conceived, designed, built and tested with unprecedented speed. It swept the 1964 Daytona 500 race and has endured as one of the finest V–8 automotive engines ever built. Chrysler

less been the case for some years, but it was made explicitly clear when rather exotic engines or induction systems made their way into cars that had no production-line counterpart that could be verified, and NASCAR would immediately disqualify the entry.

The manufacturers shifted the research and development to street cars with racing parts available over the parts counter at the dealer. There was some under-the-counter activity between the factory and now-independent racing teams to be sure, but the major objectives by the AMA had been achieved. Thus, the late fifties and the early sixties stock-car racing was pretty much a team effort as opposed to a factory effort.

February 22, 1959, was the biggest day in NASCAR history—the first running of the 500 mile race of the newly opened Daytona International Speedway. The Daytona 500 race would play a pivotal role in the decision to implement a crash program for a new Chrysler racing engine.

The Wedge Rules

In the early sixties, the 413 Wedge was Chrysler's performance engine of note. In 1962, the company introduced the Max Wedge 413. The release of this engine was directly tied to Chrysler Corporation's new president, Lynn Townsend, who stepped up to the presidency in the middle of 1961. The company gained a new advocate of performance and racing, and the change, Hoover remembers, was almost immediate.

"When Lynn Townsend came in as president of Chrysler, the good fortune was he had two teenage boys. They were known to travel North Woodward Avenue late at night. They made it known straightaway to Dad that this stuff [Chrysler Corporation cars] was nowhere. He was highly sensitive to the fact that the product line was nowhere out there with the young people. The rationale was, you can sell an old man a young man's car but you can't sell a young man an old man's car.

"There were," Hoover continues, "encouragements from Bob McCurry over at Dodge, certainly Gale Porter, Frank Wylie from Dodge public relations, and Jack Shirapar. Jack was our champion. He was the guy who could carry the message from the trenches—from North Woodward and Detroit Dragway—right upstairs. Jack knew what had to happen out on North Woodward.

"When Mr. Townsend, by whatever mechanism, let it be known that it was time to change the image of our product, it was just like having the clouds separating and the sun shining through. Engineering division was given the directive to get some cars out there that would do the job. I was made engineering coordinator for the whole engineering division for the race program. That was in October 1961.

"A program began in October 1961 to release in the standard-size cars performance packages based on the RB [raised-block] engine, which at the time was 413 cubic inches. I'll never forget that because Mr. Townsend himself had signed the project request to initiate it, so that was like walking into engine design with a blank check.

"The first of the cross-ram, eight-barrel 413 Wedge cars we got running was a white Plymouth two-door. Mr. Townsend himself, the chairman of the board, came out to the proving grounds one day and I took the car out there. He stood out there at the east-west straightaway and had me make a pass with the car so he could listen to the car and watch it. He had the ability to understand what it meant, and I'll go to my grave believing it was his two teenage boys who put that sparkle there.

"Those [Max Wedge] cars," Hoover explains, "hit the drag race scene like an H-bomb. They just blew everything else away by eight to ten miles an hour. I think that there's no question that the experience that all the Ramchargers had gained the preceding three or four years at the drag strip and North Woodward was fundamental to making those cars successful.

"The 413 Wedge was less successful as a Grand National stock-car engine," Hoover reveals. "If the Wedges had been more successful in Grand National racing, the need for the 426 Hemi wouldn't have existed, because the Wedges were doing a good job in drag racing, and that success was related to modifying the TorqueFlight automatic transmission for drag-racing purposes. Pontiac was the job to beat at the time, if I recall correctly. It became evident that in order to really make a big splash at Daytona Beach in the Grand National cars, we needed a better level of power."

The 413 Max Wedge and later the 426 Max Wedge were Chrysler's first true high-performance racing-engine programs. The managers of these successful programs were under the direction of Bob Rarey. He had joined Chrysler in 1942 and became assistant chief engineer of engine design in 1955 when Mel Carpentier died. By the early 1960s, Rarey had become chief engineer in charge of engine, transmission and engine electrical. When asked by Bob Anderson to take over all racing-engine work at Chrysler, Rarey balked. However, he did agree to set up a separate group, apart from production-engine design, to handle this activity. The success of the Max Wedge 413 and 426 was a tribute to his foresight and support. The engines, however, could not realistically double for circle-track racing.

The reason for this was not just the Wedge-shaped combustion chamber of the 413 and 426, but the size of the intake and exhaust valves and the design of the intake and exhaust ports. While the engines performed well on the short, quarter-mile strip, the high rpm, high horsepower requirements of stock-car racing exposed the Wedge's limitation in producing the level of horsepower necessary to win.

Willem L. Weertman would become closely involved with the new racing engine that evolved. A 1947 graduate of Yale, Weertman joined Chrysler that year and entered the Chrysler Institute. After graduating from the two-year work-study program, he began work at the Plymouth Road assembly plant. When the Mound Road engine plant was built for the production of V–8 engines, he was selected as the first resident engineer of the plant. In 1955, Bob Rarey, as the new assistant chief engineer of engine design, selected Weertman to be manager of engine design.

"We had a fairly strong factory effort with the Wedge V–8 in 1962 and '63," Weertman says, "but it was obvious to those managing the program we were not competitive with it. About that time,

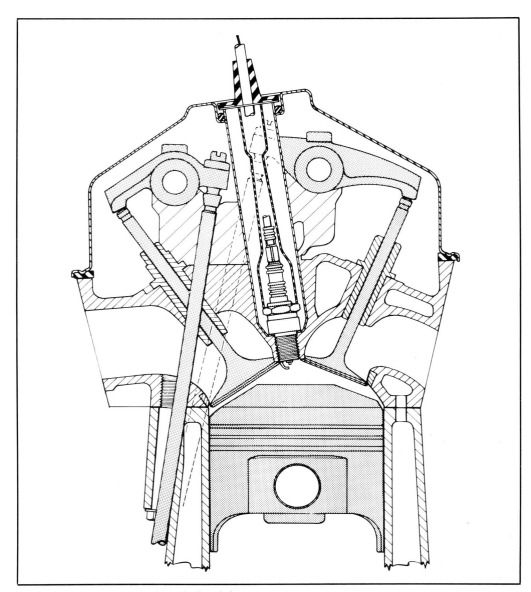

A fifth head bolt, shown here behind the intake valve pushrod, was a key feature of the 426 Hemi. Chrysler

in late '62, early '63, it was a collective decision by our race policy people, which included Bob Rodger, who said in effect, 'Either we do something big or we should get out. What we are doing is not meaningful to the company, to our dealers or to car sales.' So [Rodger], Tom Hoover and Bob Rarey had to think about what might be possible and immediately the thought came to their minds, 'Can we have a Hemi version of our B and raised-B engines?'"

Engine Code: A864

"I remember exactly where I was on the second floor of the main building in Highland Park," Hoover says. "Don Moore was there, I was there and a couple of other people. It was the winter of '62–'63, and the big Wedges had not done well in NASCAR. A couple of us offered up the argument, I suppose it was Don Moore and myself, 'If we're going to make a new head for the engine, let's go with what we know is right. We know the Hemi will do the job, and we have all the A311 and Cunningham background upon which we can rely to proceed forward.' Jack Shirapar picked up the ball and he's the one who carried it right up to the executive

The cylinder-head design of the 426 Hemi was similar to Chrysler's first-generation Hemi of the fifties.

committee. I got to carry the drawings up there for Jack. He made the pitch and Townsend didn't hesitate a bit. [He said] 'Do it.'"

The decision to put a Hemi head on the raised-block 426 was borne of necessity. Lynn Townsend wanted the new racing engine in time for the Daytona 500 race in February 1964. The Hemi design team was faced with an almost impossible deadline. Thus, the decision was made to use the same basic machin-

ing dimensions as the 426 Wedge in order to use existing tooling. Cylinder bore centers were 4.80 in. Height along the bore axis was 10.725 in. Vertical height from the crankshaft center was 10.875 in., and overall length was 23.46 in. Bore was 4.25 in. and stroke was 3.75 in.

"In March 1963," Weertman continues, "we gave that assignment to our advanced engine group under Bob Dent, and the lead designer of that

group was Frank Bialk. We were racing the 426 Wedge-head engine at the time. We had the displacement set up, now we had the challenge of trying to put the Hemi head on that engine. A critical decision was made by that group to stay with the included valve angle from the old Hemi engine, because we had a background that describes the chamber, valve sizes and the performance of the engine."

With a maximum vertical separating load of 18,800 lb. at 7200 rpm along the crankshaft centerline, durability of the bottom-end was of paramount concern. To ensure durability and rigidity, the main-bearing cap design of the 426 Wedge was abandoned.

"Steel bearing caps appeared in the early Hemi for testing Firestone tires at Indianapolis," Hoover explains. "Also, Briggs Cunningham used early Hemi engines for some road racing in Europe and the need for good structural support for the crankshaft bearings became evident during that program."

Bialk designed a new set of number two, three and four main-bearing caps that took advantage of the current deep-skirt walls of the raised-block by adding cross-bolts that went through the block walls into the bearing caps. This enabled the engine-block skirt structure to aid the bearing caps to resist the horizontal loads pushing the cap across the engine. This cross-bolt main-bearing cap design used ½–13 bolts vertically through the bearing cap to the block and ⅜–16 bolts horizontally through the block skirt to the main-bearing caps. Later in the 426 Hemi's development, these were increased to ⁹⁄₁₆–12 and ⁷⁄₁₆–14 bolts, respectively.

The cylinder head was a unique design challenge for a number of reasons.

"One thing that we had on the new engine that was better than the old engine was the headbolt pattern," Weertman says. "Our B and raised-B engines had a five-bolt headbolt pattern as compared to four on the prior engines. The ability to clamp the head is crucial to how much you are ever going to get out of the engine. The problem that we faced in doing the Hemi became the solution that made a real engine out of it: how to handle the fifth headbolt. The fifth headbolt was literally in the way of the pushrods and intake port. This area would be so restricted it wouldn't have much more power than the Wedge-head engine. What Frank Bialk came up with was to bring the bolt up from underneath. It took him awhile to be sure that, indeed, we could bring a bolt up from underneath."

The juxtaposition of the intake and exhaust valve within the combustion chamber was also crucial. If the two valves were equidistant from the bore centerline in the transverse view, the resulting engine would be so wide it couldn't fit into the cars it was designed for. It also resulted in an exhaust-valve rocker arm of alarming proportions. The solution was achieved by rotating the included valve angle of 58 deg. across the hemisphere toward the intake manifold.

"We looked at that rocker arm and that thing kept looking like a huge pump handle," Weertman laughs. "We reduced its length until we thought, 'That's going to work.' That set where the valve was going to be. We had daily meetings on the board to see what Frank had, then we'd let him work for several days to come up with his best thinking. He was really an amazing guy. He would say whenever he would get into a corner, 'Sometimes I just go home and I'll have a vision. I'll come back to work and [it will be] just fine.'

"That was part of the challenge of getting the chamber design in place," Weertman continues, "to come up with just the right compromises on the top-end. The use of the rocker shafts was sort of ordained because of their use on the prior-generation engine. It was a sturdy arrangement, with forged-steel rocker arms."

Once the design for the cylinder block and heads was finalized, these two long-lead items were procured for manufacture. Chrysler's American Foundry Division in Indianapolis, Indiana, was chosen for casting the cylinder block. Campbell, Wyant and Cannon Foundry Company in Muskegon, Michigan, was selected to cast the cylinder heads. Weertman explained how Chrysler was able to get these new engine parts into production so quickly: "We took the production [426 Wedge] parts, making just the changes we needed to. Where we could, we would take an existing box, or pattern, and change it. We were able to go from our prototype design to the first casting quickly. However, many

The 426 race Hemi used these steel-tube and cast-iron flange headers. The tube pattern on the right header was distinctly different from that on the left. Chrysler

The connecting rod was designed to withstand a separating load of 18,000 lb. at 7000 rpm. Chrysler

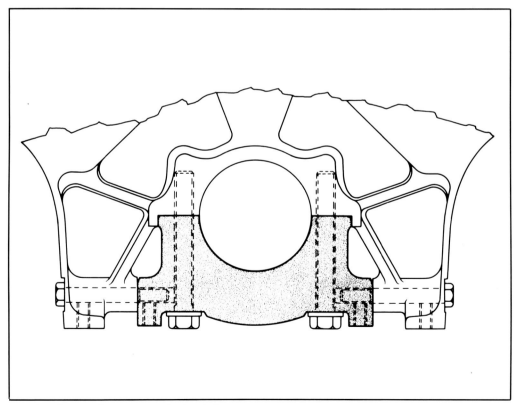

Another key to the 426 Hemi's durability was the use of cross-bolted and recessed main bearing caps.

The 426 Hemi for NASCAR events in 1964 and 1965 used a single Holley four-barrel carburetor on a dual-plane high-riser intake manifold. Chrysler

The intake manifold designed for sanctioned drag racing was a plenum-ram design with staggered dual four-barrel carburetors. Chrysler

parts, like the cylinder heads, did require all-new equipment."

When the 426 Hemi engine was given the go-ahead for development, the decision was made to have a parallel design program for a drag-racing Hemi. Thus, two distinct intake manifolds were designed by Forbes Bunting at Chrysler. The circle-track single-four-barrel intake manifold was a dual-plane design for use with a Holley carburetor. The drag intake manifold was a plenum design with two staggered four-barrel carburetors. Each carburetor sat atop a plenum chamber that fed the four cylinders on the bank opposite the carburetors. The Carter carbs on the drag manifold used $1^{11}/_{16}$ in. primary and secondary bores with a rating of 770 cfm (cubic feet per minute). The track-engine Holley carburetors used the same primary and secondary bore diameters. Both intake manifolds were cast aluminum.

Reciprocating Parts

As originally designed, the pistons would be impact extruded from an aluminum slug. To achieve the 12.5:1 compression ratio required for the track and drag engine, the top of the piston was contoured to protrude 0.755 in. into the combustion chamber. Valve timing at top dead center—the end of the exhaust stroke and beginning of the intake stroke—resulted in both valves being partially open. This required circular depressions in the top of the piston to permit 0.070 in. clearance between the valve and the pistons.

The connecting rod would go through two redesigns at the crankshaft end, but initially it used two $^7/_{16}$ in. bolts loaded to 16,300 lb. each—close to their yield point. The rods were forged. The distance between the piston pin and crankshaft bores was 6.871 in., with a minimum I-section of 0.35 sq-in.

The crankshafts for both the track and drag engine were identical in dimensions but made of different materials. Main journal diameter was 2.75 in. Crankpin journal diameter was 2.375 in., and the stroke was 3.750 in. Undercut journal fillets were incorporated, as in the previous Hemi. Initially, all journals were finished to 0.015 in. but later were reduced to 0.015 in. to prevent oil film breakthrough under high rpm. The circle-track crankshaft was forged from SAE 4340 high-strength alloy steel; the drag-racing crankshaft was forged from SAE 1046 carbon steel. Both cranks then underwent the same finishing procedure. They were first heat treated, then machined, with the exception of the finish grind on the journal surfaces. After being entirely shot-peened, the journals were ground. The entire crankshaft was then surface hardened by a nitride-immersion process call Tufftride. Finally, the journals were lapped.

The mechanical camshafts for circle-track and drag racing differed also. The 1964–1965 track camshaft had an intake and exhaust duration of 312 deg. with 88 deg. of overlap and 0.54 in. of valve lift. The 1964 drag camshaft had 300 deg. of intake and exhaust duration with 76 deg. of overlap and 0.52 in. of lift.

The valvetrain was designed to withstand the punishment of flat-out racing. The valve angle from bore centerline was 35 deg. for the intake valve and 23 deg. for the exhaust valve. Intake valve diameter was 2.25 in., with a hefty 0.309 in. diameter stem. The 1.94 in. diameter exhaust valve had a stem diameter of 0.308 in. Dual valve springs were needed on each valve, requiring 384 lb. to fully open. A spiral spring damper was placed between the inner and outer spring.

Forged rocker arms featured full-length steel-backed bronze bushings. The rocker-arm valve tip was hardened and ground to 0.030 in. These rocker arms were adjustable, using a 3/8–24 UNF thread with a locknut.

The rocker-arm shafts had an outside diameter of 0.872 in. and an inside diameter of 0.60 in. The rocker shaft was hardened at the location of each rocker arm. Light helical springs were necessary on the shaft to keep the rocker arms in place against the adjacent brackets.

Malleable-iron rocker-shaft brackets were attached to the cylinder heads using five of the cylinder head bolts. A solid dowel accurately located each bracket. Holes were drilled in the brackets to permit oil to flow from the bracket mounting surface to each rocker shaft.

Valve tappets were mechanical, made from extruded steel and having a brazed-on iron face. The pushrods were made of steel tubing, 0.375 in. in diameter with a heft 0.083 in. wall thickness. Hardened-steel inserts that contacted the tappet and rocker arm were pressed in and then welded to the ends.

A 426 Hemi undergoing assembly. Test engines were assembled in Chrysler's Highland Park, Michigan, engine lab. Production racing engines were assembled at Chrysler's Marine and Industrial division in Marysville, Michigan. Chrysler

View of the assembled 426 Hemi cylinder head. Note the CWC foundry mark of Campbell, Wyant and Cannon Foundry Company. Chrysler

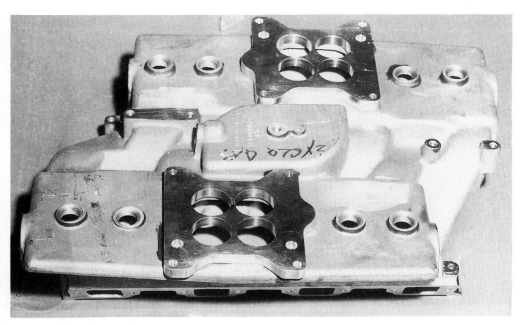

A drag-racing intake manifold after machining. This intake manifold was also used on Chrysler's famous 1968 Super Stock Barracudas and Darts, which are still campaigned today. Chrysler

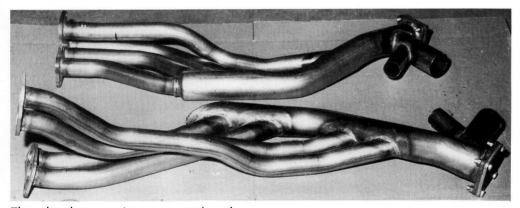

These header extensions were used on the 426 race Hemi and incorporated the use of cutouts where rules permitted. Chrysler

Chrysler also designed new exhaust headers for the 426 Hemi. The headers were made from 2 in. diameter steel tubing, welded to cast-steel flanges which bolted to the cylinder head. Initial dynamometer testing resulted in 45 in. tube length before discharging into a 4 in. collector. Subsequent testing showed an improvement in high-end power when the tubes were shortened to 30 in. and mated to a flange plate, to which undercar header extensions were

42

bolted. The configuration of the four exhaust-header tube centers differed for the left and right. In addition, the tubes on the left exhaust header were grouped to one flange, while the ones on the right of the engine had two separate two-tube flanges.

Machining and Assembly

The raw cylinder blocks and heads were shipped from their respective foundries to the Trenton, Michigan,

engine plant for machining. Changes were made to the 426 Wedge-block line to allow for the Hemi's requirements.

"Trenton could put the blocks down their main machining line," Weertman says, "and then they had offline operations for the block, for example, to put in [the main-bearing cap] side bolt holes. Trenton was giving us virtually hour-by-hour service on the blocks. I was in touch with the factory manager, and he understood our desire. Of course, he had his own production schedules to meet. We challenged them to do this whole job quickly because the corporation had almost no time to get the job done."

Although the production 426 street and race Hemis were to be assembled at Chrysler's Marysville, Michigan, engine plant, the test and early racing engines were assembled at the engine labs in Highland Park. The Hemi parts shipped there from the Trenton plant underwent minute inspection and checking before being approved for final assembly.

"Prior to building each engine," Troy Simonsen relates, "we did a lot of dimensional checks. We Zyglowed the pistons to look for cracks, and we Magnaglowed the blocks, the cranks, the rods and the heads. Steve Baker and I had the responsibility of the day-to-day, nuts and bolts—was the engine holding together?—and analyzing and testing anything that required mechanical development. We supervised and wrote the orders for building up all of the engines, which included all of the ones that went to the Daytona race."

Steve Baker joined Chrysler in 1960 and entered the Chrysler Institute. He had the good fortune to be assigned to the engine lab that would eventually oversee assembly and testing of the 426 race Hemi. With so much riding on the success of the Hemi, it was essential each engine was assembled with great care.

"Our only secret here," Baker says, "was that we took extreme care in cleanliness and making sure the parts were good. It took about eighty man-hours to assemble a race Hemi, not counting the machining time. Most of that time was in inspection, checking all the parts to make sure they were within tolerance. Things like taking a white cloth through each cylinder bore, not just to make sure they were clean, but to make sure the assembly guys understood this was the way it was done."

Chrysler had no previous experience testing an engine designed purely for circle-track racing. Weertman called in Larry Adams, in charge of the race Hemi engine testing program.

"I said to Larry, 'How do we find out if our engine's going to be durable enough for Daytona?' We had durability schedules for testing passenger-car production engines—long 800 hour tests. We didn't have any durability schedules for our racing engines."

Weertman and Adams came up with the idea of running the engine testing in the lab identical to the demands made on the engine during an actual 500 mile race, including straightaways, banked turns and pit stops.

The first 426 race Hemi build-up started the last week in November 1963 and was ready for lab testing the first week in December. The Daytona race was only two months away. Before putting the new engine through its race-profile testing, the engineers thought it prudent to bring it up to speed slowly to establish power readings in the dyno room.

"At the time," Baker remembers, "that room had a 400 horsepower Amplidyne dynamometer. Well, we knew we had a hell of a lot more horsepower. There were several of us there—the operator, myself, and the department manager, Ev Moeller. So we slide-ruled the observed power. We got 400 horsepower around 4800 rpm. There was a possibility we were going to break the dyno. Moeller was in charge and said to go ahead. He would take responsibility so the operator wouldn't get into trouble for damaging equipment. As I remember, we got up to more than 425 horsepower the very first run we made with the engine—and the dyno didn't break. Everyone was pretty pleased with that."

Preparation for Daytona

This engine, and others, then began their rigorous race-profile testing, and the dyno rooms in Highland Park reverberated with the unmuffled roar of 426 Hemis running at full power. With the Daytona 500 qualifying races just a few weeks away, the pace at Chrysler reached a fever pitch. The prestige of Chrysler Corporation was riding on the 426 Hemi and it was a make or break situation. Yet, for many of the engineers and technicians, these months of frantic

A fully assembled 426 drag Hemi, minus only the air cleaner, with manual four-speed transmission. This configuration was offered in Chrysler's 1964, 1965 and 1968 factory drag cars. Chrysler

effort are the most memorable of their careers.

"Some of my fondest memories," Simonsen recollects, "would be coming to work in Highland Park very early in the morning before daybreak in the winter. We were running three shifts of operators with the dynamometer crew. The engines ran headers with an exhaust system that dumped into a six or twelve inch stack that then went up and exhausted out over the roof on the third story of the building. As you came across the parking lot at 5:30 in the morning, it just echoed all over Highland Park."

Problems arose quickly, however. Weertman co-authored a 1966 SAE paper with Bob Lechner chronicling the saga of the 426 Hemi's development, and the first problem encountered would prove the most nerve-racking.

"Shortly after the first engines were run at full power," Weertman and Lechner wrote, "several engine failures occurred due to vertical cracks in the thrust side of the right hand bank bore walls. A quick analysis showed that these block cracks were occurring in the bore wall opposite the piston pin pier.

"A reduction of this load concentration could have been obtained by increasing the piston cam so that the bore wall would be loaded more uniformly by adding load to the center of the bore while reducing it at the crack location area. The piston, however, had just undergone an intense development program of its own and further changes to it were ruled out."

"We were bringing the engine up to as much power as we could get out of it with this deadline of the Daytona race in February in front of us," Weertman says. "It was in fairly quick succession that they found cracked cylinder bores in the lab engines. I was in my office when Larry Adams, who was in charge of race engine development, came into my office, just sat down in the chair and said, 'Bill, that engine isn't going to last. We

In 1966 Chrysler offered a new intake manifold for NASCAR competition. Chrysler engineers nicknamed it the Bathtub intake manifold. Chrysler

aren't going to finish the race.'

"I told him, 'Well, Larry, what's it going to take?'

"'We have to thicken up the bores. There's really no other way.'

"I said, 'OK, we'll see what we can do.' The date was January 28, 1964.

"What we did on the board," Weertman reveals, "was we made a template that could be used to take an existing water jacket core at the foundry, scrape it away and as we scraped the sand away, we would add metal to the block. So we made up these templates to give the thickness in the areas we thought would do the job. We handed them off to our foundry liaison who worked in engine design by the name of Louie Taylor. He flew down to the Indianapolis foundry where the blocks were being cast. He took with him another man—Earl Pinches.

"Louie took the templates we had

set up and he attempted to scrape some cores and get the cores ready to make castings, but the cores cracked apart. We took away so much sand, that he couldn't get a good core. He called from Indianapolis and said, 'Bill, we can't get any good cores with these templates. You're going to have to come here and help me.' So, at that point, I flew down to Indianapolis and I saw that we had added too much metal to the bore walls to solve the cracking problem, but now we couldn't get a block casting. We then proceeded to file a number of cores in batches of twelve cylinder blocks which required both the right- and left-hand cores. We did these by hand with modified templates so the foundry could reproduce this, because at some time Louie, I and Earl Pinches were going to leave that foundry, but we would want them to continue to make good blocks for us.

"We put the cores through their normal process, which requires a core wash, then the core is dried out before it's put into the mold and the casting made. We had worked late on a whole bunch of castings and we went back to

the motel to get some sleep, and the people called us from the foundry and said, 'All the blocks are scrapped that came out.' We went back to the foundry and the blocks were missing large segments of the metal. We had a giant mess on our hands.

"The foundry people were really cooperative. They were doing whatever we wanted them to do. We looked at it and we got our heads together. They said, 'What we think happened is that those cores were not baked out enough and that there was still water retention in the cores.' When those cores went in the mold and when the iron went into the mold and hit the moisture, it blew the metal away, and we were seeing voids in the metal.

"We went through the process again, and I think we went through that about three times. The whole process took about three hours, from scraping the cores, processing them, putting them in the mold, pour the iron, and let the iron cool down before going through shakeout before we got a casting at the other end. We were so anxious to know if we had a good block, we just kept at it. We indeed worked twenty-four hours straight. We were totally exhausted, but we finally came out with a block that looked like a sound casting. We had several blocks and we said, 'Ship it!'"

The date was February 3, 1964. Three blocks from this group would be in the final race. These blocks, however, were not shipped directly to the engine plant for machining. They were shipped first to a stress-relieving furnace for a reheat and slow cool-down. This was done because, along with the bore-wall cracking, bulkhead cracking was also found during engine testing. Considering the substantial design of the Hemi block, the consensus at Chrysler pointed to this being a problem of residual stress in the block casting and not to a design problem. The stress lab and the metallurgists went to work on it. Oscar Willard began work in Chrysler's stress lab in 1956, and remembers well the problem with the 426 Hemi block.

"We worked as a service group almost exclusively in the stress lab," Willard says. "Anytime a problem arose in the corporation from a strength standpoint with failures involved, they usually came to our area to get help to determine what the cause of failure was and what had to be done to remedy it. I worked with some pretty brilliant people and I was at the working level. The problem was presented to them, and the engineers and technicians would stress analyze the blocks.

"We were heavily into residual stress back in an era where it was an art more than a science. There was so much that was unknown about metallurgy: how it reacts when it is poured, where does the residual stress come from? The time after pouring the metal until it is taken out of the mold and cleared of sand is very crucial.

"We were working around the clock in the stress lab along with the people who were running the dynos," Willard says about the 426 Hemi's pre-Daytona 500 race development. "We had prepared an engine block, heads—anything that was having problems. We had completely strain-gauged the block, and that meant bringing the wires out of the crankcase so that we could get to them and hook them up to the electronics. We worked in shifts around the clock for the whole weekend when we were having this crisis. We would come in for our eight-hour shift, compile the data and give it to the next shift, and by Monday morning we had all the answers. We got in the think tank and the decisions of what had to be done were based on that. This was within two weeks of the Daytona race."

With the data and recommendations from the stress-lab engineers in hand, the foundry received new instructions to eliminate the 426 Hemi's residual stress. All previous core preparations and casting procedures were followed. After cool-down and shake-out of the sand core, with care to ensure all sand was removed so as not to allow a temperature concentration, these blocks were placed in a large furnace and reheated to 1,200 deg. Fahrenheit to relieve the blocks' internal stresses. Then the furnace temperature was slowly lowered before the blocks were removed and shipped to Trenton for machining, then to Highland Park for assembly into engines.

Car testing had already been started with the original-design Hemi well before the dyno testing was completed. Steve Baker remembers the first vehicle test with the 426 Hemi.

"The first track test we did with a Hemi in the car," Baker says, "was at the

Straight-on view of Bobby Isaac's Charger Daytona shows off the car's sleek aerodynamics. The car was slick enough that Isaac had earlier set a closed-course record, running a similar car up to 201.104 mph. Isaac allowed how the car was so stable, any driver could turn 180 mph laps straight off the showroom floor. Dr. John Craft

Goodyear track at San Angelo, Texas, with Ray Nichols and his crew. Paul Goldsmith was the driver, and he complained the track was kind of rough. We went out and you could see where the car had become airborne and then came down, leaving tire marks. We had timed him at 180 miles per hour. This was the very first time the 426 Hemi was installed in a stock car."

The date for check and pre-race

inspection for the Daytona 500 race was February 4, 1964. Engines had been built and shipped to the teams ahead of this date to give the teams time to make the car installations and to start their own preparation and testing. These engines, of course, were the original design. The gamble had to be taken that these engines would hold up long enough to get through practice, the qualifying laps and the qualifying races. Then the miracle had to happen: beginning with the new, heavy-wall castings that American Foundry started making on February 3, the blocks had to be machined, built into engines and delivered to Daytona in time for all the teams to change their engines before race day on Sunday, February 23, 1964.

As the first engines were built and shipped to the racing teams for installation in their Dodges and Plymouths, there was a secret among all of them that was never revealed to anyone else. The Hemi could develop power that would put the other cars to shame, but Chrysler didn't want to tip its hand. Troy Simonsen explains what that secret was.

"When we went to Daytona in '64, Ford had been dominating the race and Chevy had had the 'Mystery Chevy' engine the year prior and had done very well with that engine; it was the quickest engine on the track at that point. Chrysler had been getting beat regularly. We weren't much of a contender. Of course, NASCAR wants to have a good show, and they wanted three participants.

"We were coming out with the Hemi, and the NASCAR rules were essentially that it was to be a production engine in a production car. We intended that this was going to be a production engine in a production car, but at the time we went to NASCAR we didn't have any production cars out there. We were able to convince NASCAR—who wanted to be convinced because they wanted another participant—that it was going to be a production car in the spring, two months later, which we did make. We knew Ford was going to object if we were really wild and tough, and they would lean on NASCAR not to say it was a recognized production car, so we were careful when we went to Daytona.

"During the weeks of qualifying and getting the cars ready," Simonsen reveals, "we never, during that time, did a wide-open lap. Never. Junior Johnson was one of our drivers. He had driven the Mystery Chevy engine the year before and he said it was just unbelievable the amount of difference in the power between the Mystery Chevy engine and this [Hemi] engine. Going down the back stretches, they would lay their foot in it and feel what it did, and they would feel what it did in the corners, but they never, ever made a complete lap wide open, because they didn't want somebody in the stands timing them and finding out they were eight or ten miles an hour faster than Ford. We were turning 170 mile an hour lap times just like the Ford guys were doing. It looked like it was going to be a good race. NASCAR was happy and everybody was getting comfortable with the fact that we were there. That was the whole plan."

Plan or not, the drivers couldn't resist using enough of the Hemi power to set new course records. On Friday,

February 7, 1964, Paul Goldsmith qualified with a two-lap average of 174.91 mph. Richard Petty qualified at 174.418. The next day two fifty-mile pole position races were held with half of the qualifiers in the first race and half in the second race. Goldsmith won his race at an average of 170.94 mph. Petty won his at an average of 171.99 mph. With his original qualifying speed, Goldsmith won the pole position, with Petty on his right, for the Daytona 500.

The rest of the starting positions were determined in two 100 mile qualifying races held on Friday, February 21, 1964. Junior Johnson won the first race with a speed of 170.777 mph. Bobby Isaac won the second race at 169.811 mph. Every one of these speeds broke prior records.

Not everything went according to plan, however. The qualifying races served to put the Hemi through actual racing conditions, even if the engine was not being run flat out. Yet another weakness had surfaced during the qualifying races.

"In the car that Junior Johnson drove," Simonsen says, "the engine finished the race with twenty pounds of oil pressure. We knew what we were going to find without tearing the engine down. The block cracked right down the oil line between the cam and the main-bearing bulkhead."

The fears about the durability of the first cylinder blocks had been underscored.

Two days after the fifty-mile pole position races, a ladle of molten iron at 2,600 deg. Fahrenheit was poured in a mold at American Foundry. This casting would become the cylinder block of the engine that was destined to win the final race.

As each heavy-wall, stress-relieved block arrived at the engine labs, assembly of the Daytona 500 426 Hemi engines began with all the other, pre-inspected

The Dodge Charger Daytona dominated NASCAR's superspeedways throughout the 1969 and 1970 seasons, and Bobby Isaac drove the K&K Insurance car to victory at many of the venues. His sponsorship was irony at its peak; while K&K sponsored this NASCAR racer, the whole muscle-car era would soon be doomed due to the insurance companies' excessive rates on similar performance cars. Dr. John Craft

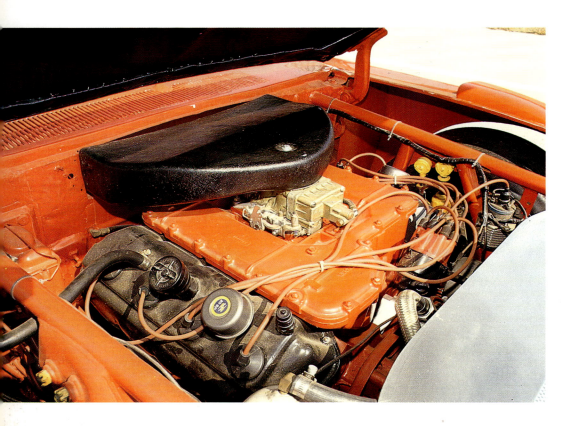

The 426 race Hemi of the Isaac NASCAR Daytona. The large airbox plenum fed the single carburetor through the air slots at the base of the windshield. Dr. John Craft

Previous page
Rear spoiler of the Isaac Daytona, photographed along pit row on the Talladega, Alabama, superspeedway. The Daytona inherited the flush-mounted rear window from its predecessor, the limited-production-run Charger 500. The giant spoiler was all its own. Dr. John Craft

parts to expedite assembly. The assembled engines were painted, then sent to the dyno labs for performance confirmation. Each engine was then bolted to an engine stand for transportation to the waiting racing teams at Daytona.

Millions of dollars had been spent to develop the 426 Hemi, and there were fears about sending the engines by plane. Oscar Willard remembers with bemusement this crucial next step to the hoped-for Daytona 500 win.

"I remember we had a bunch of skeptics here," he laughs. "I asked a question once and they said, 'They're building an engine over there in the motor room right now, and they're going to be sending it down to Daytona tonight, so make sure if there's anything you have to add that it's included.'

"'They're shipping it down tonight?' I asked.

"'Oh yeah. They've got a truck waiting for it.'

"'Truck? Why don't they put it on a plane and fly it down? Why don't they take two at a time?'

"'What if they have a plane crash?'

"The thinking was, at the time, they did not trust the plane. The mechanic from, say, Petty's crew, would come up here, pick up the completed engine, drive it down there, throw it in the car and they'd be testing it the next day. They couldn't stand the thought of shipping two in an airplane at one time because there was such a scarcity of the parts."

Bob Lechner was assigned the task of taking additional 426 Hemis to Daytona, with the added bonus of watching the race.

"I took three or four Hemi engines down to Daytona in a pickup truck with another fellow," Lechner says. "Most of the major racers already had theirs; these were strictly spares. I had tickets in the grandstands area. It was the first time I had ever seen a Grand National race."

The 1964 Daytona 500

February 23, 1964, dawned cool but sunny. As the stock-car fans filled the stands, there were countless discussions and bets as to who would win the race and what make would take the checkered flag. The qualifying races gave the best indication and determined the starting line-up. Out of a starting field of forty-six cars, the first seven positions were Dodges or Plymouths.

Paul Goldsmith held pole position in his Plymouth Belvedere. Next to Goldsmith was Richard Petty in his number 43 Plymouth. Junior Johnson was in third position, driving a Dodge Coronet. Bobby Isaac was in fourth, also driving a Dodge Coronet. In fifth position was Buck Baker behind the wheel of a Belvedere, as was Jim Pardue in sixth position. David Pearson was in seventh, driving a Dodge Coronet. Jim Paschal was in tenth position driving a Coronet. The race program stated these cars were

Hemi Engines at 1964 Daytona 500

Cylinder block	Casting date	Car number	Crew	Driver	Final position
0726	2-10-64	43	Petty	Petty	1
0688	2-7-64	54	Burton and Robinson	Pardue	2
0704	2-10-64	25	Nichols	Goldsmith	3
0583	2-3-64	5	Owens	Paschal	5
0641	2-5-64	3	Fox	Johnson	9
0589	2-3-64	41	Petty	Baker	12
0586	2-3-64	26	Nichols	Isaac	15
0647	2-6-64	6	Owens	Pearson	DNF

powered by "Chrysler Corporation's Hemispherical Combustion Chamber Maximum Performance Engine."

The miracle had happened. Every one of these cars was powered by a new, heavy-wall Hemi engine. The race teams had done their part in making the engine changes the day before the start. Chrysler, and the teams, were ready to race.

Ronnie Householder, Chrysler's director of stock-car racing, was in the pits, making sure the pit crews had the needed fuel, tires, parts—and spare 426 Hemi engines. As the official 12:30 pm start of the race approached, the field of cars began their pace laps.

"Ev Moeller and I were in the stands across from the pits," Bill Weertman smiles. "They started off and I don't know how many laps it was, maybe twenty-five or fifty laps, [when] the cars came into the pits and the hoods went up! We just about died. That was a sign that you've got trouble. What happened was there was so much paper and debris on the track, that it was being sucked up and plastered on the front of the radiators, and the engines were overheating. What they had to do, of course, was get all this stuff cleared off the radiators. Down went the hoods, off they went onto the track, and they really dominated the race."

That day racing history was made and a legendary engine was born. Three hours and fifteen minutes later, Richard Petty was first across the finish line followed by Jim Pardue and Paul Goldsmith—a one-two-three sweep by Plymouth. Jim Paschal was fifth, seconds behind the leaders. Junior Johnson was ninth. Hemi cars set a new average speed record of 154.334 mph.

"Ford had had a major ad campaign with the slogan, 'Total Performance,'" Troy Simonsen remembers fondly. "Within days after taking first, second, third and fifth at Daytona and having dominated that race, everybody here, on the teams, in the lab and in public relations was wearing a little button that said, 'Total What?'"

Chrysler president Lynn Townsend was jubilant. Chrysler had not only won the most prestigious stock-car racing event in NASCAR, it dominated the top finishers. Townsend immediately looked for other fish to fry, and looked to

The interior of the Bobby Isaac Daytona is all business. The essential gauges are mounted in a simple, lightweight, fabricated dash. Dr. John Craft

Indianapolis. He called Bob Rarey into his office.

"'We've wiped those guys out of Daytona, now let's wipe them out of Indianapolis. Build an engine that will take care of them at Indianapolis,'" Rarey remembers Townsend telling him. "So we designed a small-displacement Hemi engine. Townsend came to me and said, 'I've just gotten the cost figures on this thing. We're going to go racing with those guys, but it's going to cost $7 million. You've got to tell me what our chances are to win.' I said, 'I don't know what kind of a racer you are or how many races you've been to, but if you've

ever seen an Indianapolis race, there are thirty-three cars in the race and some of them don't make it through the first turn. I would say since there are thirty-three cars in the race and we have two of them in there, we'll have about a one in sixteen chance.' And he said, 'For seven million dollars, we're cancelling the program.' So, we never built that one."

The Woodward Avenue Race Shop

Chrysler's fledgling race group was faced with a corporate structure that was not experienced in building the race cars needed to get the job done. The development of the 426 Hemi for NASCAR and sanctioned drag racing made that clear. There was no convenient place to do prototype development cars at Highland Park. In order to do the job professionally and avoid corporate red tape that would slow pro-

Dick Landy established a colorful and enduring reputation for himself racing Hemi-powered Dodges during the sixties. With cigar clenched firmly in cheek, he comes off the line in one of the first factory Maximum Performance Package 426 Hemi Charger Dodges, racing in Super Stock/Automatic. Dick Landy

gress, a separate facility had to be found.

Dick Maxwell joined Chrysler in February of 1959 and graduated from the Chrysler Institute two years later. He joined the Ramchargers and immediately began working in the race group on Chrysler's drag-racing efforts. It was clear to Maxwell, as well as others in the race group, that they needed a place to build their test cars.

"There was really no place inside engineering where we could do the sort of things we wanted to do," Maxwell says. "We needed a specialized facility where we could do prototype race cars, or whatever."

After some searching, Hoover felt he had found the ideal building: an old Pontiac dealership on Woodward Avenue that had gone out of business. Its location was appropriate, too. Woodward Avenue had become the street to cruise—and race. It had developed a mystique and was known to enthusiasts all over the country.

Dan Mancini was put in charge of running Chrysler's new race-car shop. Mancini had joined Chrysler in 1953 as a driver and mechanic, and quickly moved on to the dynamometer lab. Later, he was responsible for engine build-up for the engines that were tested in the lab. This was followed by work in the carburetor lab. It was while working there he learned of the Ramchargers and became involved. Hoover chose him to supervise the running of the garage.

Mancini gathered a crew of five mechanics from within Chrysler with a keen interest in racing and skill in engine building and car fabrication. They were Roger Lindamood, Larry

The *Little Red Wagon was one of the wildest applications of 426 Hemi power seen during the sixties. With its built-in wheel-standing capability, it routinely set elapsed times in the low tens at speeds over 125 mph.* Chrysler

Knowlton, Fred Schrandt, Dan Knapp and Ted Macadaul.

"This was where we built the racing mules for testing," Mancini says, "whether they were for drag racing or NASCAR. Tom Hoover and Jim Thornton supervised the drag cars and Larry Rathgeb handled the stock cars."

The 426 Hemi Drag Cars

It was the production of the 426 Hemi-powered drag cars that ostensibly made the Hemi a production engine. How many engines constituted a production engine? Curiously, this was a nebulous point with NASCAR, and no engineers at Chrysler today can remember any definitive minimum production run specifically requested by

54

NASCAR for homologation. Bill Weertman and Bob Lechner, however, did state in their SAE paper roughly how many 426 drag-race Hemis Chrysler built.

"Immediately following the initial introduction of the engine," they wrote, "a production run of several hundred drag racing engines and cars were planned to be built. The production of the several hundred drag engines was completed by the end of the 1964 model year. Another production run of several hundred drag engines was made for the 1965 model year automobiles, with a considerable weight decrease for the engines obtained by use of aluminum and magnesium components."

The Dodge and Plymouth factory drag cars truly were set up for the strip. The 12.5:1 compression ratio 426 Hemi was factory rated at 425 hp at 6000 rpm, but to racers who knew better, this rating was obviously conservative. The standard rear-axle ratio was a Sure-Grip 4.56; optional ratios available ranged from 2.93 to 5.38. Dual Carter AFB four-

barrel carburetors sat atop the short-ram aluminum intake manifold. The cars came standard with the TorqueFlight three-speed automatic transmission. The A–833 four-speed manual transmission was optional.

Dodge called its Hemi the Dodge 426 Hemi-Charger. In its booklet Dodge added this disclaimer in bold type to discourage any would-be racers from taking the car to the public streets:

"The Hemi-Charger 426 engine is designed for use in supervised acceleration trials and other racing and performance competition. It is not recommended for general every day driving because of the compromise of all around characteristics which must be made for this type of vehicle. In view of its intended use this vehicle is sold "As Is" and the provisions of Chrysler Corporation's manufacturers passenger car warranty or any other warranty expressed or implied does not apply."

In the booklet section describing features, it stated a lightweight aluminum front-end package was available as optional equipment for better weight distribution. This included aluminum fenders, hood, dust shields, front bumper, bumper-support brackets and doors. Door glass and front quarter window winders were replaced with plexiglass and the window winders were eliminated. The rear window was replaced with 0.08 in. tempered glass. The hood was fitted with a large air scoop to feed colder, denser air to the angled, oval air filter spanning both carburetors.

"The Super Stock drag-race cars were intended only for drag-strip use," states Troy Simonsen, "but were production-built cars and we built a lot of them, both manual and automatic. They had a minimum amount of equipment in them. You could take one out the door, put a set of M&H tires on it, uncork the headers and go turn 11.50."

Naturally, this was *the* vehicle of choice for the Ramchargers and they did extremely well with it. At the American Hot Rod Association (AHRA) Summer Nationals, the Ramchargers achieved an 11.06 sec. elapsed time in the quarter-mile at 132.62 mph, seizing the Top Stock Eliminator title. At the National Hot Rod Association (NHRA) Nationals in Indianapolis, where the Hemi blocks had been cast, the Ramchargers set an NHRA record of 11.23 sec. at 130 mph in the Super Stock class.

Racing Parts Procurement

A key facet in the 426 race Hemi story is the procurement of parts. It's one thing to design and manufacture the parts, but once made, how did they get to the engine lab for assembly and testing and to the racers themselves? The product lines of Dodge, Plymouth and Chrysler had their own system for procuring parts, but the race group had no such system; one had to be created. The man responsible for setting up the racing parts procurement system was Brian Schram.

Schram joined Chrysler in 1949 as a clerk at the Dodge plant. In 1955, he had the opportunity to join the product engineering office at Dodge, building new-car prototypes and procuring the parts. By 1960, he was working for Gale Porter and Frank Wylie, ensuring parts supply to Carl Kiekhaefer and Lee Petty. Through Porter, Schram began to help Robert Cahill in Dodge's drag-racing program, procuring parts first for the Max Wedge 413 and 426 and then for the 426 Hemi. The Ramchargers also turned to him to meet their racing parts needs.

Schram established a parts depot at Dodge's Product Planning Lynch Road garage. He operated the depot by himself at first, systematizing everything from the air cleaner to the oil pan and every part in between. As the 426 Hemi stock-car and drag-racing programs mushroomed, Schram was assisted by Gene Carr, Dave Johnson and Mo David.

Notification of a parts requirement would come to Schram via a memo, usually from an engineer affiliated with the race group. "For example," says Schram, "Dick Maxwell would send me a Speedi-memo stating, 'Send Sox and Martin two Hemi cylinder heads,' or something like that. I'd crate the parts and take them to Detroit Airport for shipment to the racers."

Schram says the stock-car racing parts program was structured differently. Race-car builder Ray Nichols, under contract to Ronnie Householder in charge of Chrysler's stock-car racing program, would receive the parts from Schram; the parts were not sent directly to the racing teams themselves.

Twin-Cam and Aluminum Hemis

Chrysler did not sit still with the 426 Hemi's development. The corporation rightly surmised GM and Ford would

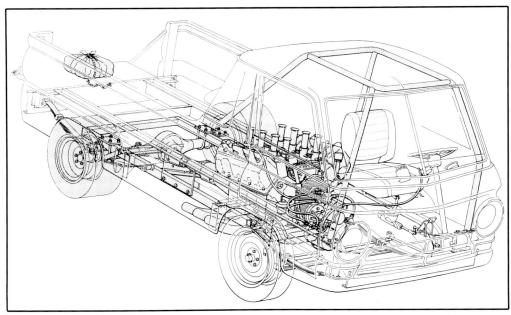

The Little Red Wagon *took shape in* Chrysler's Woodward Avenue garage. Based on the Dodge A–100 compact pickup, the 426 Hemi with Hilborn fuel injection was bolted into a rugged new frame to add strength to the pickup's unibody. Bill "Maverick" Golden campaigns the Little Red Wagon *to this day.*

Dick Landy got one of the six 1965 Dodge altered-wheelbase factory drag cars designed to compete in A/FX class drag racing. Dick Landy

Stock-car driver Bobby Isaac piloted his 426 Hemi-powered Dodge Daytona to twenty-eight national and world records on the Bonneville Salt Flats, Utah. Chrysler

redouble their efforts to beat the Hemi.

"After the first several races [in 1964]," Simonsen recalls, "Ford made a major drive and improved their performance of both the engines and the cars, and from then on out, the races were pretty much competitive."

One of the designs intended to improve the 426 Hemi was the A925 engine program. This was a double-overhead-camshaft design with four valves per cylinder. A prototype was built, and although it never ran in Chrysler's dyno labs, this prototype served an important purpose.

"Ford went down to Daytona for 1965 with their racing engine," Rarey says, "which wasn't a Hemi exactly but was darned near, I guess. They said they wanted to race *that* against us. Ronnie Householder went into Bill France and said, 'Hey, look fellows. If you run that Ford engine, we're running this engine.' He takes the cover off it and shows the

four-valve Hemi. This engine had a sixteen-branch intake manifold. It was unbelievable. France just said, 'As of now, the Ford engine isn't running and neither is *that*.' We eliminated the Ford competition with that one engine."

Unfortunately, the NASCAR ban on the Ford single-overhead-cam 427 and Chrysler double-overhead-cam 426 Hemi also extended to the 426 Hemi they were currently racing. Although Ford and Chrysler filed protests, Bill France did not waiver. Chrysler withdrew its factory support for the 1965 season. Ford, however, took advantage of the void left by Chrysler and opted to race its mass-produced 427 ci Wedge-head engine. Many Dodge and Plymouth stock-car drivers, faced with the NASCAR Hemi ban, shifted their efforts to NHRA, AHRA and USAC (United States Auto Club) sanctioned events in 1965. Richard Petty, for example, raced a Hemi-powered Barracuda in B/Altered.

One of the Hemi engine programs that did see the light of day was the A990 program, originally an offshoot of the A864 Hemi program. Ways of reducing the weight of the 426 Hemi for drag racing were studied. Bill Weertman made

his first entry regarding the program in his monthly progress report dated June 2, 1964: "A reduction in power plant weight has been effected by use of aluminum and magnesium parts." In his progress report of July 29, 1964, he wrote: "The first aluminum cylinder head was cast on July 24. The cast was almost perfect with only one small area of porosity. Changes to eliminate this porosity are being made. Additional castings will be made on July 28 and July 29, 1964."

In August 1964 the lightweight 426 Hemi engine program officially received the A990 designation. The new parts included aluminum cylinder heads, oil-pump body, oil-pump cover, water-pump housing, water-outlet elbow and alternator bracket. The intake manifold was cast in magnesium. The aluminum heads were first cast by Alcoa and later by various small foundries around the country, one of which was Ross Foundry in Ohio. The magnesium intake manifold was cast in California and the machining was performed by Keith Black.

Other changes for the A990 Hemi included increasing the exhaust branch manifold outside diameter from 1.88 to

Miss Chrysler Crew *was an unlimited hydroplane powered not by the usual Rolls-Royce or Allison aircraft engine but by two supercharged 426 Hemis. The boat was campaigned by Bill Sterett in the late sixties.* Chrysler

2.00 in., and the switch from Carter to Holley carburetors.

In his progress report dated August 25, 1964, Weertman announced the production schedule: "The production volume of this engine will be 210. The production build schedule is: First Car—11-16-64; Last Car—1-8-65."

After the first A990 was run by the dyno lab, only four minor changes were necessary for production to begin. These were use of copper head gaskets instead of steel, thicker head bolt washer, longer head bolts to accommodate the thicker washers and increased length of the chrome plating on the valve stems.

The A990 Hemi was installed in some of the wildest factory-built drag cars ever offered by a major car manufacturer. The most radical Chrysler offer-ing to date was built for the Altered/Factory Experimental and Ultra/Stock classes. Dodge shortened the wheelbase of its Coronet by moving the front wheels and rear axle forward for vastly improved weight transfer. The hood, doors and trunk lid were made of fiberglass. Dick Landy was among many of the drag-racing greats who bought and raced these cars.

"Those cars," Mancini recalls of the A/FX drag cars, "turned out to be a little bit too light. We had taken a lot of strength out of the car when it was acid-dipped and as a result, on a very hard acceleration you could actually bend the car. So we had to go through another program to strengthen the car with a rollcage and a couple of bars underneath."

With Chrysler absent from the high-banked ovals for the first half of 1965, Bill France was once again faced with a dominant factory presence—in this case, Ford. He contacted Henry Banks, director of competition for USAC. The outcome of their discussions was a NASCAR bulletin released to the press on June 15. The joint agreement covered rule changes affecting both sanctioning bodies for the remainder of 1965 and 1966. The rule changes pertaining to NASCAR were: "(1) A minimum weight limit of 9.36 lbs. per cubic inch of displacement for a car ready to run with a full load of fuel, oil, and water. For example: a car with a 427 cubic inch engine must weigh 4000 lbs. (2) The Hemi engine will be permitted on NASCAR tracks of over one mile in the 1965 Dodge 880, and 1965 Dodge Polara. All 1964 Dodges competing on these tracks must use the wedge-type engine. (3) The Hemi engine will be permitted in the Plymouth Belvedere and the Dodge Coronet on all USAC and NASCAR tracks of one mile and less and road courses."

France and Banks also announced that in 1966 a joint committee composed of USAC and NASCAR officials would categorize all American production cars. The four categories were standard, intermediate, compact and sports. For 1966, intermediate-size cars, such as the Plymouth Belvedere and Dodge Coronet, would be permitted to race on oval circuits of more than one mile with a 405 ci limit. In a statement that seemed directed at the Chrysler 426 Hemi and

Ford sohc 427, Banks said, "One of the objectives of the committee will be to eliminate the high cost/low volume engine from competition."

This was a moot point. Chrysler had already decided to make the 426 Hemi available in Dodge and Plymouth passenger cars for 1966. Consequently, the Hemi wasn't eliminated from competition, but it did have to conform to the displacement-reduction rule.

To meet these new rules, Chrysler started the A117 program. This Hemi had a shorter 3.558 in. stroke requiring a new crankshaft and longer connecting rods with 7.174 in. center to center. Displacement was 404 ci. To offset the inevitable loss of power, the two key areas studied were the intake manifold and camshaft timing.

Hemi Variants

John Wehrly joined Chrysler in 1962 and the Ramchargers shortly thereafter. After working in the area of engine cooling, he moved on to the engine development lab. In 1971, he became race engine development supervisor. The intake manifold for the 1966 404 ci circle-track Hemi was a new approach involving extensive development.

"We developed a single four-barrel manifold we called the Bathtub manifold because it dipped down in the center," Wehrly says. "The purpose was to get the hood clearance down and still have the length of the runners we needed. The longer runners in that type of intake manifold were a real challenge—to have a manifold that had good driveability because of all the sharp angles and the fact that the air had to twist through the manifold. We did a great deal of work on that design, looking at dozens and dozens of manifolds."

The camshaft was even more radical than the one used in the A864. Intake and exhaust duration was now 328 deg., with 112 deg. of overlap and 0.565 in. of lift.

A number of variations of the 426 Hemi were pursued by Chrysler which never saw production. One of the first was a spin-off of the A990 program called the 300 Hemi. This was a serious consideration to provide the Chrysler 300 Letter Series luxury sport sedan with Hemi engine power in addition to its Wedge engine. Since the engine would be somewhat detuned for street use, the block and bearing cap structure would

be made more like the production 440 Wedge engine. This would make it easier to produce at the Trenton Engine Plant.

In a November 2, 1964, program memo, Weertman described the proposed 300 Hemi alongside the A990 Hemi. This engine had a larger 4.32 in. bore with the same 3.75 in. stroke, resulting in 440 ci. The block was to forgo the lengthy and expensive heat treatment and would not have the cross-bolt main-bearing caps, opting for the less-expensive standard two-bolt main-bearing caps. Other concessions for the street included a 268 deg. hydraulic camshaft, single instead of double valve springs and new, less costly exhaust headers. The hot induction setup included three two-barrel Carter carbs on an aluminum intake manifold—a precursor to the Six-Pak that would appear in 1969. Effort was made to install an air-conditioning compressor on the engine. Sadly, the 300 Hemi remained a proposal and nothing more.

Another race Hemi design was the A148. On December 2, 1965, a Performance Planning Letter initially requested a variant of the A864 with a larger 4.363 in. bore and shorter 3.558 in. stroke to allow for the use of larger valves. Intake valves were 2.44 in. in diameter and the exhaust valves were 2.06 in. Longer valve springs were used to permit greater valve lift. Flow testing of the prototype cylinder head early in 1966 proved this design flowed better than the A864 but not as well as the double-overhead-cam A925. Both iron and aluminum cylinder heads were procured for this 426 Hemi. Engines were built and tested, but says Wehrly, "What we really found was that so much development was required to get the same reliability that we didn't pursue it any further."

Dyno Testing: "Good Luck Guys"

The pace of Hemi design development and testing throughout the sixties never slackened, as Chrysler worked to keep up with the ever-changing NASCAR rulebook and performance gains by its competition. Ted Flack joined Chrysler in 1967 and landed a job that 426 Hemi enthusiasts dreamed about.

"I was 20 years old and wanted to go racing. I figured if I could get into a car company, I could learn more—the se-

crets of this engine stuff," he remembers. "So I walked into personnel and asked, 'Have you got any openings for mechanics?' And they said, 'Yes. We have one here in the dynamometer section.' They brought me around and walked up and down the dyno buildings. They were running a couple of Hemis—racing engines. I felt like a kid in a candy store.

"When I was working there, there were six guys in the motor room just building Hemi engines. Many times we'd put an engine on a dyno stand while the paint was still wet. Then, after a power run, we'd have to back off to deliver it to somebody for a race and the engine would still be hot when we loaded it onto a truck. When they would ship engines for a race, they would write notes on top of the manifold like, 'Good Luck Guys.' When it came time for the race, the guys down there would send up reference charts, so we knew which engine was in which car and the guys here who built it would know which car actually had his engine."

The dyno labs literally performed destructive testing on the 426 Hemi to learn its limits as well as confirm performance. Explosions were unpredictable because of the test cycle and the number of hours on an engine. When a Hemi finally came apart under the most grueling test conditions, the results were spectacular.

"We had them blow up," Flack recalls, "where there was nothing on the stand—the crankshaft would be on the floor, the heads blown off into the corner. One fellow here had a picture where one engine actually sawed itself in half. The back half was gone and the front half was hanging there by the radiator hose. There are holes in the ceiling down there still to this day.

"The back side of the dyno cell used to be all windows. When we'd run the engines, the headers would glow red. A lot of guys would stand and look in the windows to see what we were doing, sometimes with their face pressed against the glass. It wasn't really safe because you never knew what was going to happen. One day, we shut down the engine, went outside and told the guy, 'We don't want you standing right by the window.' He left, we brought the engine back up to speed—about 7000 rpm. Thirty seconds later the engine blew up. Complete connecting rods went through the window right where he had been standing. One landed out in the driveway, still sizzling, and burned a hole down into the asphalt."

When NASCAR tightened the screws again requiring a restrictor plate using 1⅛ in. bores, the dyno lab was crucial in surmounting this supposed problem.

"We came up with a venturi-effect spacer about two inches high," Flack says, "and actually made more power with it than we did without it—about fifteen more horsepower."

Power gains came from new camshafts with ever-increasing valve lifts that were possible with the higher valve springs that had been started with the A148 program. It was also decided to change from a chain-driven camshaft to a gear-driven camshaft to eliminate any camshaft rotational fluctuations caused by chain flexing.

A flat crankshaft was tried. The theory was to improve power by always alternating exhaust pulses from one bank to the other rather than having adjacent cylinders fire, as is the case with a conventional V–8 crankshaft. The problem was that the engine was no longer in balance and the secondary forces shook the engine. There was so much trouble with bolts loosening and parts breaking that it was finally decided that the power gains, if any, weren't worth it.

The 1968 Super Stock Cars

The most awesome application of the 426 drag Hemi came with the introduction of the 1968 Hemi Dart and Hemi Barracuda. The Woodward Avenue garage had seen some wild Hemi-powered prototypes built there, and conversations often drifted around the garage of stuffing the 426 Hemi into Chrysler's two smallest cars—the A Body Dodge Dart and Plymouth Barracuda—for use in Super Stock class drag racing.

"Dick Maxwell was a fundamental champion of the Hemi A Body," Hoover says. "I can remember at the time I argued that we should keep the Hemi in the B body because that's where we sold to people, but I'm glad that Dick prevailed because by many standards, they are the world's nastiest, meanest production cars that people could go out and buy."

The 1968 Super Stock program was the most ambitious Chrysler had under-

Dick Landy tests his new 1968 factory Super Stock Hemi Dart at Irwindale Raceway. Chrysler contracted with Hurst Performance to build seventy-five Dodge Darts and seventy-five Plymouth Barracudas powered by the 426 Hemi drag engine. Many of the surviving cars are still raced today. Dick Landy

The engine bay of Dick Landy's 1968 Super Stock Dodge Dart. The power-to-weight ratio of these cars permitted them to dominate their class for years. Dick Landy

59

As this photo shows, the mold for the twin-plug cylinder head was not modified to accept the second spark plug. Several machinings converted the single-plug head to the twin-plug design. Chrysler

taken up to that time, but the procedure for getting corporate approval and funding was the same as previous race-car programs.

"We usually had to get sales division approval to do something like this," Maxwell says. "The race group at that time was in product planning. The first thing we would do was go to the product planners and sign them up in supporting the program. Then, we'd go to our leader, Bob Rodger, and get him behind it, and then the sales divisions and sell them on it, which wasn't hard because there was so much enthusiasm for racing in those days and drag racing in particular because of the muscle-car boom. We were doing so well in that market. Once we had that done, it was a matter of scraping up money—which was sales division money—to pay for the program."

Since the Dodge Dart and Plymouth Barracuda had similar chassis and body dimensions and clearances, it was felt only one prototype needed to be built. A Barracuda was selected as the mule and shipped to the Woodward Avenue garage. Bob Tarrozi was the mechanic and engineer who first worked out all the calculations on paper, then went about extensively modifying the car to drastically reduce its weight while strengthening the car to deal with horsepower and torque levels the A-body was never designed to handle.

"That car," says Maxwell, "was the mule—the test car. Everything was worked out in that car, and the purchase order contract was let to Hurst Perfor-

mance, which opened up a facility up in Hazel Park and built the cars for us."

Stock Barracudas and Darts were shipped to the Hurst facility where the cars were modified and the 426 drag Hemi installed according to Tarrozi's manual that had been compiled from the prototype. The cars were left in grey primer so the racers could add their own color scheme. Dodge and Plymouth cranked up the public relations mill, getting the word out about Chrysler's new drag cars.

"We had no trouble selling those cars," Maxwell remembers. "We originally scheduled fifty of each, and we had so many orders we went back and built twenty-five more. We built seventy-five of each. I don't remember what the prices were but they were pretty reasonable, and they could be ordered through the dealers."

The D Cylinder Head Program

During 1969 and 1970 Chrysler undertook a cylinder head refinement program to experiment with various aspects of design that affected intake and exhaust flow. All these heads retained the hemispherical combustion chamber, but the engineers experimented with a great many ideas; the most feasible, from a manufacturing standpoint, were designated for prototype or limited production for use on the racing engines. Hemi enthusiasts know these as the D heads.

The D1 cylinder head used the same diameter intake and exhaust valves but

had larger ports. Each intake port had 3.00 sq-in and the exhaust port had 2.10 sq-in. Intake valve angle from cylinder bore centerline was 35 deg.; exhaust valve angle was 23 deg. This head was tested for the 426 race Hemi.

The D2 cylinder head was essentially the same as the D1 but used on the 429 ci displacement Hemi as permitted by NASCAR rules, using a 0.02 in. overbore. The lab engine with this setup was run in April of 1969, but the D2 program was canceled the following month because performance gains were not sufficient.

In his program report on the D3, Bill Weertman wrote, "The A864 D3 is the first of several cylinder heads designed to provide larger valves and increase flow, intake and exhaust ports." The valve angles had to be changed due to the new intake valve diameter of 2.38 in. with a 3.65 sq-in intake port, and an exhaust valve diameter of 2.00 in. with a 2.53 sq-in exhaust port. In addition, the cylinder bores had to be notched for intake valve clearance. Displacement remained at 426 ci. Two cylinder heads were prepared in March 1969, and the intake manifold modified to match the heads the following month. The first power run was made on May 9, 1969, but ironically, power was less than the D1 Hemi.

Between the D3 and the D4 cylinder head design was the D3.5. It used the large intake port of the D3 head and the exhaust port of the D4. The castings for this head were ordered in May 1969 and they were machined in the engine lab that September. No records of the flow results are available.

The original write-up for the D4 head was made May 12, 1969. In his program report for this cylinder-head design, Weertman wrote, "The A864 D4 design was made to investigate improvements for making the exhaust port higher with less curvature and with larger area." The head was ordered March 12, 1969, but the first power runs weren't made until May 1970. The 426 Hemi with D4 heads generated 641 hp on May 1, 1970.

The race group wanted to see what the D4 heads with a gear-drive camshaft would do on the Daytona Speedway, so the engine was put in the engineering test car and shipped to Daytona. The track had already been rented for May 12, 1970, just to test the car. Paul Bruns,

The 426 race Hemi was first offered in factory-built race cars in 1964. Dick Landy was among the first to get his hands on one of these cars, this one being a Dodge 330. This fully documented example is now owned by National Hemi Owners Association member Pete Haldiman. David Gooley

Dick Landy spared no expense to make this car as light as possible. Body panels were acid-dipped and frame members were drilled to reduce weight further. These steps, combined with the best production drag-racing engine ever designed and Landy's driving skill, made him one of the most successful racers in the sixties. David Gooley

manager of the engineering race-car program, and Bill Weertman were there. The car ran a lap at 191.172 mph, which was a boost of almost 3 mph over runs with a prior engine.

The D5 cylinder head was probably the most famous of all. This was a cast-aluminum twin-spark-plug design that incorporated all the improvements in the D4 design. The twin-plug feature aided flame propagation. This cylinder head actually saw limited production for use by 426 Hemi drag-racing enthusiasts.

There were other cylinder head variations on the 426 Hemi. One of the last investigated was the D20 Magna design. In his progress report on this design, Weertman wrote, "The D20 'Magna' was a design study to provide extra large ports and valves. In order to avoid a long, high inertia rocker arm, a two-piece pushrod was devised connecting with a small tappet in the cylinder head." The D20 had a 4.00 sq-in intake port with a 2.50 in. diameter intake valve, positioned 31 deg., 45 min. from cylinder bore center. The exhaust port had a 2.60 sq-in cross section with a 2.20 in. diameter exhaust valve set at 36 deg. from the cylinder bore center. With this valve geometry, the head was wider, requiring larger cylinder-head covers. The aluminum version of this design was the D21. Work progressed from its first write-up in November 1968 until May 1969, when the program was canceled

The interior of the 1964 Dick Landy drag car has been beautifully restored. The red and black interior contrasts handsomely with the car's silver paint. David Gooley

Next page
The 1964 factory drag-race cars were originally equipped with magnesium wheels. Today, those wheels have been replaced by aftermarket pieces. Bigger, fatter tires have required altering the rear suspension for proper clearance. David Gooley

There was no column shift in the big Chryslers in 1964 because the corporation was exploring the wonderful world of push-button transmissions! It was a moot point in a car like this, since Landy let the TorqueFlight do the job all by itself. David Gooley

Even more fearsome than the 1964–1965 factory drag cars were the Super Stock Plymouth Barracudas and Dodge Darts built in 1968. These cars were conceived by Ramcharger member Dick Maxwell. The prototype was executed by the able men at Chrysler's Woodward Avenue garage and the cars were built by Hurst Performance. The Barracudas, like this one, are more frequently seen today than the Darts. David Gooley

Two generations of factory race Hemi drag cars: Dick Landy's original 1964 car and the 1968 Super Stock Barracuda. These truly are historic quarter-mile machines. David Gooley

due to yet another sudden rule change by NASCAR.

That rule change ended further 426 Hemi development and production for racing. The rule change was a result of the exotic, aerodynamic body designs that hit the high-banked ovals in 1969 and 1970. For Chrysler, greater performance gains were achieved through aerodynamics than by further horse-

power development. The first Mopar to reflect this thinking was the Charger 500, followed by the Dodge Daytona and then the Plymouth Superbird. Once again, Bill France put the brakes on these and other aero stock cars by requiring a maximum displacement of 305 ci powering them. This rule was to take effect for the 1971 season. This was too drastic a change to make altering the Hemi worthwhile.

"Actually, the manufacturing of the [race] Hemi stopped before the racing," Wehrly says. "The last batch of iron heads were cast around 1970. The last aluminum heads were cast in the early seventies."

Although production had ceased, Chrysler continued to offer technical support to the thousands of devoted 426 Hemi racers. Keith Black, Milodon and others took up the 426 Hemi and offered it in aluminum. A new generation of Hemi enthusiasts was guaranteed to continue the 426 Hemi's long, record-setting history.

Next page
Factory Super Stock cars were finished in a primer grey and owners painted their cars after taking delivery. This Super Stock Barracuda has been painted a pale yellow. When first raced, it was covered by sponsor decals. David Gooley

Previous page
The incredible speed with which the 426 race Hemi was conceived, designed, tested and built makes the enduring success of

the Super Stock Barracuda and Dart even more amazing. After a quarter of a century of competition, these cars are still virtually unbeatable in their class. David Gooley

James Hylton, number 42, charges through turn 9 at Riverside, California, in his 426 Hemi-powered Superbird. The aerodynamic Plymouth Superbird and Dodge Daytona signaled the twilight of the 426 Hemi in NASCAR events. Chan Bush

Ed Miller of Rochester, New York, traveled across America to compete in the NHRA Winternationals at Pomona, California, with his Hemi Plymouth Super Stock. Chan Bush

The Ramchargers pioneered the use of
superchargers on the 426 Hemi, and every
other drag racer soon followed suit. Chan
Bush

The 426 Hemi was campaigned by the
Ramchargers into the seventies. Here,
Leroy Goldstein pilots his 1971 Challenger
funny car. Chan Bush

Sox & Martin were among the most familiar names in drag racing in the sixties and seventies with their red-and-white 426 Hemi Plymouths. Here, Ronnie Sox is behind the wheel of their 1971 Hemi 'Cuda, racing in Pro Stock at Pomona, California. Chan Bush

Judy Lilly raced Miss Mighty Mopar in SS/AA. The Plymouth 426 Hemi Super Stock factory drag car remains the high-water mark in a long line of Chrysler race cars for the quarter-mile. Chan Bush

426 Street Hemi

Ruling the Road 1966–1971

The factory rating for the street Hemi of 425 horsepower was right on. When we did a scuff test, we'd fire up a green engine—no hours on it—and run it at max horsepower for two hours. Those things made 425 horsepower like clockwork.

—Ted Flack

For years, automotive enthusiast magazines have stated the 426 street Hemi was offered for sale to meet minimum production requirements by NASCAR and other sanctioned racing organizations. This is partly true, but other factors were involved in turning the 426 Hemi loose on American streets.

Early on, Chrysler looked into offering the 426 Hemi in passenger cars during the 300 Hemi program. To make the 426 street Hemi affordable, expensive steps in the engine's manufacture were to be deleted and modifications made to civilize the Hemi for street use. But the proposal went no further.

The idea of putting the 426 Hemi in street cars was not as outrageous an idea at the time as one might first believe. It was, after all, the performance era, and every car manufacturer was offering high-performance, large-displacement engines—some with multiple carburetion—in their passenger cars. Chrysler had offered Hemi-head engines in their cars before, and they were touted for their greater performance compared to Ford and General Motors. For 1964, Chrysler offered a new 365 hp 426 Wedge in its Dodge and Plymouth models, and the 426 race Hemi was offered in

When a dark paint scheme was ordered on a 1970 Hemi 'Cuda, the graphic identification was white, above. Left, in 1970, only 72 Plymouth GTXs with the optional 426 Hemi were built. David Gooley

those Dodges and Plymouths for sanctioned drag racing.

In light of all this, it is easier to understand Chrysler's decision to detune the 426 race Hemi and make it an option in select models. What Chrysler perhaps did not know is that the 426 street Hemi was destined to become the most desirable high-performance engine ever bolted into a passenger car.

During the latter months of 1964, product planning meetings were held by Chrysler management to discuss the feasibility of offering the 426 Hemi in their cars. On January 6, 1965, Bob Rodger, special car manager and chief engineer, and Robert Cahill issued a Product Planning Letter with the title: "Hemi Performance Option Super Stock and 'A' Stock Competition." It was specifically addressed to J. C. Guenther, manager of Styling Administration and H. R. Steding, executive engineer of Engineering Administration. The models affected were 1966 model-year Plymouth and Dodge B Series cars with B and C Bodies. This letter was actually a change to an earlier performance engine proposal and gave the following description of change:

"Because of continued requirements for an ultimate performance drag

Willem L. Weertman posing with the 426 street Hemi in April 1966 when he presented the SAE paper co-authored with Bob Lechner. Chrysler

5. Pistons—Forged acceptable and thermally controlled preferred.

6. Manifolding and camshaft to be designed to give best high speed power possible while still maintaining a reasonably drivable vehicle for summer and winter.

7. Automatic and four-speed [manual] transmissions required (4-speed to have development priority).

8. No air conditioning required for 'B' Series.

9. Limited warranty is acceptable for 'B' Series usage."

Projected production volume stated in the letter was 5,000 to 7,500 cars, to take effect for the 1966 model year. The letter closed with this statement: "This engine to replace eight barrel wedge requested in Product Planning Letter... dated 8/5/64."

With the release of the January 6, 1965, Product Planning Letter, events moved quickly to make the 426 street Hemi a reality. On January 12, 1965, W. J. Bradley issued a product description of the street Hemi, now having the designation A102. It listed all the preliminary findings of additional changes that had to be made to the 426 race Hemi for use in street cars.

Race Hemi in Street Clothing

The only changes to the cylinder block anticipated were mounting lugs on the side of the block for engine mounts in C-bodies, and some machining of the mounting areas.

The crankshaft was identical to the drag-race Hemi, made of SAE 1046 carbon steel and Tufftrided. It would be fitted with a heavy inertial vibration damper.

While the connecting rods were the same as those in the A990 Hemi, the pistons were new forgings designed to produce 10.25:1 compression ratio, so that the engine could run on extra-premium fuel available at many service stations. This piston was a floating-pin design that incorporated a bushing in the small end of the connecting rod.

The camshaft, of necessity, had to be designed to develop the power expected, yet make the car drivable for street use. Intake and exhaust valve duration was 276 deg. with 52 deg. of overlap. Lift for both valves, according to the SAE paper published by Weertman and Lechner in April 1966, was 0.46 in. The camshaft drive used the same

strip, and street type engine with expanded usage, the following change in the engine lineup has been agreed upon after discussion with the affected areas.

Please release a hemispherical combustion chamber engine for 'B' Series with the following general characteristics:

1. Intake manifold to have two four-barrel carburetors.

2. Cylinder block to maintain cross tie bolt main bearing caps.

3. Cast iron exhaust manifold.

4. Solid lifters are acceptable but not preferred.

This was the stuff of which mighty Mopars were made. The Plymouth GTX was among the mightiest, and with the 426 Hemi it was as comfortable on the quarter-mile strip as it was on the street. This car is owned by Ken Funk of Los Angeles, California. David Gooley

Identification on the 1970 GTX extended to the sides of the car over the bogus scoops. There was no 426 Hemi identification on the sides of the car when that engine option was ordered. David Gooley

The performance styling of the 1970 GTX
was subdued, with no clear visible markings
revealing the fact that a 426 Hemi was
under the hood. When the accelerator was
floored, the Air Grabber hood scoop would
pop up out of the hood. David Gooley

With the hood of the 1970 GTX raised and the air cleaner removed, the inline dual four-barrel carburetors commanded attention. The Plymouth fresh-air induction system was called the Air Grabber. The operating components of the Air Grabber system can be seen under the hood. David Gooley

Next page
From a distance, there was no indication to the unwary that a 426 Hemi lurked under the hood of this Dodge Coronet R/T. Chrysler Corporation had a way of turning its standard passenger cars into muscle cars with the use of striking exterior and interior colors and scoops to drive home the performance message. When the light turned green, the Hemi took over. David Gooley

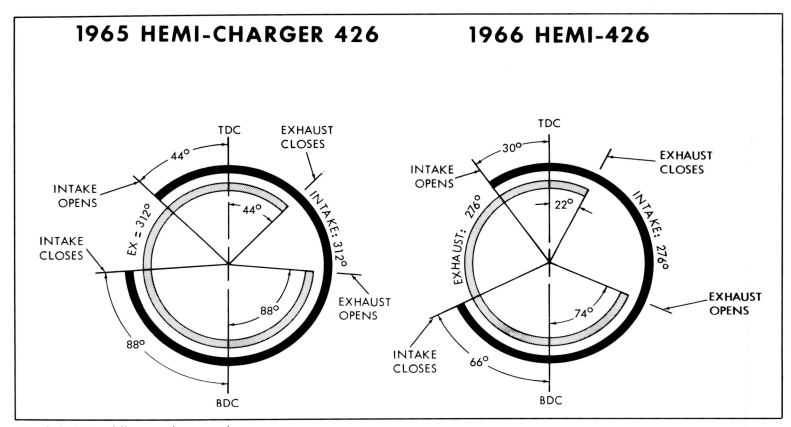

1965 HEMI-CHARGER 426   1966 HEMI-426

Camshaft timing differences between the 1965 racing Hemi and the 1966 street Hemi.
Chrysler

double-roller timing chain as the race Hemi. The 1964–1965 racing engines originally used a single 7/16–14 screw to bolt the camshaft sprocket to the camshaft, but this was changed to three 3/8–16 screws for both racing Hemis and the new street Hemi.

The valves, rocker arms, mechanical lifters and pushrods were from the A864 race Hemi, but the valve spring rates were lowered to avoid premature wear and limit engine rpm to keep rated output to the desired 425 hp.

The cast-aluminum intake manifold was a dual-plane design to use two Carter AFB four-barrel carburetors mounted inline. The front carburetor was model

A pre-production 426 street Hemi was fitted to a partial chassis in Chrysler engineering to check for clearances and possible interference problems. The valve covers on this engine do not yet have the black crackle-paint finish that would appear on production street Hemis.
Chrysler

The magnificent 1971 Hemi 'Cuda. The Hemi went out with a bang, with huge billboard graphics announcing to those with bad eyesight that ol' King Kong was under the hood. Chrysler

A TorqueFlight automatic transmission is shown bolted to a pre-production 426 street Hemi in a full chassis. Note the front suspension torsion bars. Chrysler

number 4139S. The rear carburetor was model number 4140S and, unlike the front carb, was provided with exhaust manifold heat to facilitate engine warm-up. The right-hand exhaust manifold was fitted with two aluminized steel tubes to divert hot exhaust gases to a chamber in the floor of the intake manifold at the base of the rear carburetor to achieve quicker and smoother engine warm-up. A heat control valve on the exhaust manifold would shut off the exhaust gases to the intake manifold when the engine was sufficiently warm. A special heat shield was bolted to the underside of the intake manifold to keep engine oil from contacting the heated chamber.

The only changes to the cylinder heads were those necessary to accept the new, streamlined cast-iron exhaust manifolds; these manifolds were designed to have a long service life, as the racing exhaust manifolds, made of steel tubes and cast-iron flanges, were noisier and not as durable.

To keep the 426 street Hemi properly lubricated under all street conditions, there was a new, deep oil pan with baffles. An 8 in. wide hat-section member was welded onto the chassis crossmember; this acted as a skid to protect the oil pan from damage by road obstructions. The oil pump had a larger, ⅝ in. diameter suction hole and tube.

Unlike the chrome valve covers on the racing Hemis, the street Hemi would get valve covers finished in black crackle paint. The covers had to be modified with new depressions for body drop and running clearance.

The street Hemi would have a new air cleaner and cover. It used a huge 18 in. diameter, 2 in. high paper element. As originally specified in the W. J. Bradley letter, the air cleaner was to have a black crackle-paint finish to match the valve covers, but by the time the 1966 street Hemi made its appearance, the air cleaner cover was chrome plated.

To ensure the Hemi remained cool-running, it was fitted with a high-speed water pump having a small impeller, and used a special drive belt having greater stretch resistance at high engine speeds.

It was fully anticipated that street Hemis would see a lot of competition at

the drag strip, so special front and rear engine mounts having higher rates would be fitted in Hemi-equipped cars.

The street Hemi was to be offered with either four-speed manual or three-speed automatic transmission. The competition four-speed manual transmission was modified in a number of ways for street/strip use. A new cast-iron clutch housing was made for use with new 11 in. discs. The pressure plate was made from pearlitic malleable iron. The clutch cover and release lever were made from thicker, 0.14 in. stock steel, and wear strips were placed behind the centrifugal rollers. A new flywheel-and-ring-gear assembly was bolted to the crankshaft using eight bolts. This four-speed manual transmission designation was A833.

The automatic transmission was a heavy-duty A727 version TorqueFlight. It would use a 10¾ in. high-stall-speed converter, with a governor moving the shift points up to 5500 rpm under maximum acceleration. This transmission used five discs, instead of the four used in the standard TorqueFlight. The second gear band was increased from 2.00 to 2.50 in.

Vehicle Modifications to Accept the 426 Hemi

Due to the size of the 426 Hemi, the right front shock absorber tower in the B Bodies required modifications. The power brake-cylinder booster had to be moved to clear the valve cover. However, according to Bradley's letter, the booster would have to be removed entirely for removal of the number-seven spark plug or the valve cover for valve adjustment. The left valve cover was modified to clear the battery and battery tray. Also, on C-bodies, a dash panel depression was required to clear the right valve cover.

Due to the air cleaner's size, the hood hinge torsion bar position and support bracket had to be modified. On B Bodies, the dash panel in the area of the heater motor depression required a change for proper valve cover clearance, and the heater hose routing and fittings had to be changed, also for valve cover clearance.

Electrical wiring needed to be changed too. It was thought that shielding of the starter wiring harness might be needed. Manual transmission cars required a remote-mounted starter sole-

noid necessitating special wiring.

Finally, underneath the car would be a new dual exhaust system designed for the 426 Hemi. It used 2½ in. exhaust pipes running to canister mufflers, with 2¼ in. outlets.

On January 29, 1965, a powerplant memo was released. It consolidated previous letters and memos regarding the street Hemi and authorized appropriate design and drafting to begin. Titled "Chassis–Powerplant Design Release Memo," it affected all bodystyles except station wagons. Under "Action To Be Taken" the memo read:

"Approval has been given Product Planning's request for the release of a new 426 cu. in., 2–4 bbl., Hemi-head street package for 'B' and 'C' Series. The 'B' Series package has been designated as the A102 program and will be offered as a special equipment engine option on all 'B' Series Belvedere, Coronet, Plymouth, and Dodge models except station wagons. Because of the timing involved, this engine option is to be handled as a late product package."

This meant that production of cars with Hemi engines would begin later than the normal start of model-year production in August.

The memo continued: "The 'C' Series version (i.e., 1967 model year) of this street package has been designated as the A103 program and usage will be expanded to include Chrysler sedan models. In addition, several engine revisions such as the incorporation of hydraulic tappets and thermal-controlled cast pistons are intended, and air conditioning is desired for 'C' Series 'B' and 'C' Bodies."

The memo clearly stated that at that phase of product planning, it was envisioned Chrysler would offer the street

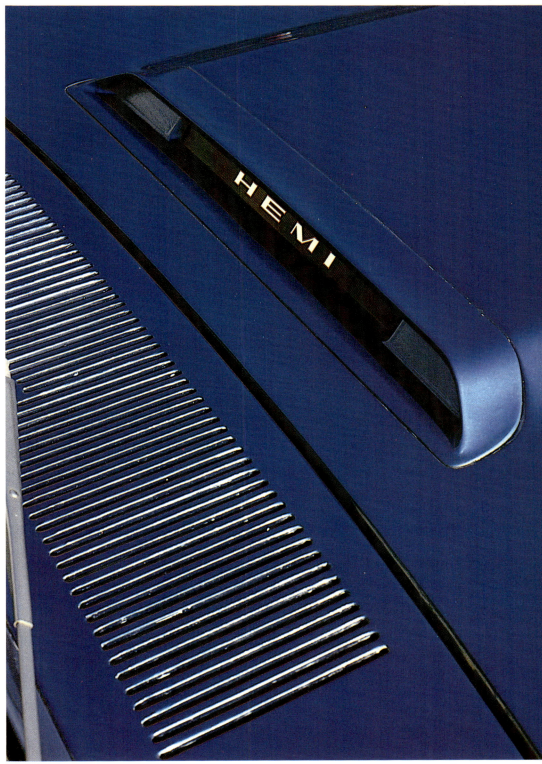

Plymouth designers never missed a chance to have some fun when they had the opportunity. The Air Grabber graphic on the sides of the pop-up hood scoop is just one example. They took performance seriously but not too seriously. David Gooley

The only Hemi identification on the 1970 GTXs so-equipped was the word Hemi at the back of the hood bulge, facing the driver. David Gooley

This production 426 street Hemi on a display stand shows the system to provide exhaust manifold heat to the intake manifold using heat riser tubes, and heat control valve to provide faster warm-up and smoother operation. Chrysler

Hemi package as an option in full-size Dodge, Plymouth and even Chrysler cars. During the early months of 1965, this was dramatically scaled back. It was decided to initially offer the 426 Hemi in the new Dodge Charger and the Plymouth Satellite for 1966.

With the introduction of the street Hemi, the famous Maximum Performance Package race Hemi cars that had been offered in 1964 and 1965 would be canceled. This made sense because the new street Hemi could be raced stock or modified to compete in the class desired by the racer.

In September 1965, the Chrysler Corporation Engineering Office issued a publication titled, "Chrysler Corporation's 'Hemi–426' for 1966." It was meant to give a complete description of the street Hemi in response to countless requests from magazine editors, newspapers and interested individuals. In part, the publication read, "Because of the increased demand and popularity, the hemi-head engine is now available as a regular production option for 1966 Plymouth Belvedere and Dodge Coronet. Belvederes powered by this high performance option are identified by the emblem 'HP2' on the fenders, Coronets by the '426 Hemi' medallion."

Initially, the HP2 emblem on 1966 Hemi-powered Plymouths raised the obvious question, What does it mean? It meant High Performance Plymouth. While the Dodge medallion was to the point and self-explanatory, the Plymouth badge was curiously vague. After several months' production, the HP2 medallion was replaced by the 426 Hemi emblem.

A supplement to this publication dated November 22, 1965, listed some changes and recommendations. The TorqueFlight-equipped Hemi cars now received a supplementary oil cooler mounted ahead of the main radiator to cool the transmission fluid. Optional front disc brakes were still in the works and would be available as a factory-installed option soon. The supplement went on to give recommended oil, and the changing interval for both engine oil and transmission fluid.

Building the 426 Street Hemi

The 426 street Hemi was assembled at Chrysler's Marine and Industrial division in Marysville, Michigan. The street Hemi went through its own pre-production testing program almost as tortuous as the race Hemi. These tests were run to verify its rated output and determine its durability.

Horsepower ratings of the day were always the topic of conversation and speculation. The enthusiast magazines debated where a given engine was grossly overrated or deliberately conservative. It turned out the factory rating of the 426 street Hemi was literally truth in advertising.

"The factory rating for the street Hemi of 425 horsepower was right on," Ted Flack recalls from his days in the dynamometer labs. "When we did a scuff test, we'd fire up a green engine— no hours on it—and run it at max horsepower for two hours. Those things made 425 horsepower like clockwork."

To enthusiasts familiar with the racing Hemi, the beauty of the street Hemi was knowing the engine underwent the identical manufacturing and assembly procedures as the circle-track and drag-racing engines. This had to be the case because the 426 Hemi Dodges and Plymouths now available in Chrysler showrooms truly were street/strip machines. Chrysler could not afford to suffer reliability problems with this engine which had achieved such notoriety in NASCAR, NHRA, AHRA and USAC competition. It had to uphold the Hemi's racing heritage. Chrysler maintained this level of excellence by constant quality control.

"I remember when that engine went to the Marine & Industrial area," Oscar Willard says. "We had continuous checking for them. From every batch of blocks they received over the years from the foundry they would usually send one or two of them into Highland Park, strain gauge them, then cut them up with a big bandsaw into minute pieces to determine residual stress level in that batch of blocks."

Selling the 426 Street Hemi

With all the excitement surrounding introduction of the 426 street Hemi, the automotive magazines couldn't wait to get their hands on a 426 Hemi Charger, Coronet, Belvedere or Satellite. *Car Life* was one of the premier high-performance car magazines during the muscle-car era and tested a Hemi-powered 1966 Plymouth Satellite with Torque-Flight automatic transmission. The performance figures were 0–60 mph in 7.1 sec. and the quarter-mile was covered in 14.5 sec. at 95 mph. However, a 1966 Plymouth Satellite powered by a 325 hp 383 ci V–8 bolted to a TorqueFlight was just as quick to 60 mph. It was only at the end of the quarter-mile that the Hemi showed its abilities. In elapsed time, the Hemi-powered Plymouth was the fastest car that *Car Life* tested in 1966. But clearly, the Hemi was hamstrung with Blue Streak street tires and a closed exhaust system.

Next page
The Plymouth Road Runner was one of the most clever and memorable cars from the muscle-car era. It was meant to be a low-buck performance car and came standard with a 383 Magnum V–8. However, if cost was no object, you could order the optional 426 Hemi. This one is from 1969. Musclecar Review

A production 426 Hemi bolted to a Chrysler heavy-duty four-speed manual transmission. Dipstick was thermally shielded to protect it from exhaust manifold heat. Chrysler

Another view of the same engine. This photo shows the air cleaner with a matte silver finish. Production air cleaners would be chrome-plated. Chrysler

CAR REVIEW

The Road Runner was, in fact, as close to the stock-car look as you could get at the time, typified by the exposed steel wheels with small hubcaps. Note the small Road Runner decal above the trunk lock. Musclecar Review

The Road Runner was based on the Belvedere, and the interior remained unchanged to keep the Road Runner affordable. The leather-wrapped steering wheel is not stock. Musclecar Review

This Road Runner's engine compartment is filled with the 426 Hemi and functional Air Grabber fresh-air hood. On Hemi-equipped Road Runners, there was a

unique Coyote Duster decal on the air-cleaner cover. The guys at Plymouth obviously had fun designing their performance cars. Musclecar Review

The 426 street Hemi received its namesake color: Hemi Orange. With its contrasting black engine pieces, it visually stated that it was all business. Chrysler

The 426 street Hemi truly was a racing engine in street clothing. The cross-bolt for the first main-bearing cap can be seen just above the oil pan. Chrysler

Bert Bouwkamp has an amusing story of a private test of a new Hemi-powered Coronet.

"When I was Chief Engineer for Dodge," Bouwkamp remembers fondly, "I got a request to host Tom McCahill of *Mechanix Illustrated* at the proving grounds with a 1966 Dodge Coronet Hemi convertible. This was to be a picture session. It wasn't to involve any high speeds, so there was no ambulance like we normally have. After driving it around and having pictures taken, Tom said he wanted to take it around the oval. He wanted the pictures to show just himself in the vehicle.

"So, his associate set up the camera and Bob Ludwig and I were standing on the side. The first time Tom came by we thought he was going pretty fast. The next time we knew he was wide open. He made three or four laps. Bob Ludwig was extremely upset, because this wasn't supposed to happen. But when the magazine came out, our public-relations people were really happy because there was a yellow band across the cover that read, 'Tom McCahill tests the world's fastest convertible at 144 miles per hour.' It was a wonder the top didn't blow off, it was ballooning so much."

Advertising for performance cars in the sixties was a genre that has not been duplicated since. Some of the most clever ad lines, ad copy and graphics made up the advertising of the era to draw the youthful buyer and the young at heart.

An ad promoting the 1966 Charger also featured the 426 Hemi. It pictured a Hemi-powered Charger at speed, with "Boss Hoss" and then a picture of the 426 Hemi below. The ad read in part, "Dodge Charger with a big, tough 426 Hemi up front makes other steeds look staid. Both for show and go. Charger looks beautifully quick just standing still. And the optional Hemi V-8 supplies a kick to match, with 425 muscular horses. Not a pony or a kitten in the bunch. The hot setup? You bet."

Over the next two years, *Car Life* tested two other Hemi-powered Mopars. In 1967, they tested a Boss Hoss Hemi Charger, again equipped with a TorqueFlight automatic transmission. The car reached 60 mph in 6.4 sec. and covered the quarter-mile in 14.2 sec. doing 96 mph through the timing lights. Top speed was 134 mph. The 1967 Hemi Charger had the lowest ET and the high-

*A close-up photo of the 426 street Hemi
induction system. The engine was rated at
425 hp at 5000 rpm—but 5000 rpm wasn't its
redline! Chrysler*

The 426 street Hemi as installed in a 1966 production car. The sound of those mechanical lifters in the morning was music to the Hemi-lover's ears. Chrysler

This photo of the engine compartment showed a different brake booster than the one used for the pre-production checkout at Chrysler engineering. Chrysler

This early production photo taken in the summer of 1965 showed the production chrome-plated air cleaner, but minus the 426 Hemi decal. Chrysler

est top speed of all the cars the magazine tested that year.

In 1968, *Car Life* tested a 426 Hemi Plymouth GTX. Performance was nearly identical to the Charger tested the year before. With TorqueFlight automatic transmission, the GTX took 6.3 sec. to reach 60 mph and covered the quarter-mile in 14.0 sec. doing 97 mph through the lights. Top speed was 144 mph.

In 1969, *Popular Hot Rodding* tested a pair of Chargers—one with a Torque-Flight and the other a four-speed manual transmission. The automatic car covered the quarter-mile in 14.01 sec. at 100 mph. By advancing the ignition and removing the air cleaner, the car reached the end of the quarter-mile in 13.75 sec. at 104 mph. The Hemi Charger equipped with the four-speed manual did much better. The ET was 13.60 sec. at 107.44 mph. And this was with a 3.23 Sure-Grip rear end and vehicle weight of more than 4,100 lb.!

In 1970 Chrysler rebodied the Plymouth Barracuda and introduced the new Dodge Challenger to the pony-car wars. Both of these handsome E-bodies were designed from the outset to accept the 426 Hemi. *Road Test* magazine tested a 1970 Challenger R/T with 426 Hemi, four-speed manual transmission and 4.10 Sure-Grip differential, for the June 1970 issue.

"It takes courage to specify the Hemi option in a Challenger," the editors wrote. "You must face a drive-train warranty foreshortened to six months, a whopping $1,227.50 increase in the $2,953 list for a basic Challenger V–8 to cover the Hemi and its mandatory related accessories, insurance and operating costs matched by no other U.S. nameplate except maybe a Hemi Plymouth and the certainty that no fuzz will let you pass by unnoticed.

"In return, you get power that can rattle dishes in the kitchen when you start it up in the driveway, extra attention in any service station, respect from owners of 428 Fords and SS427 Chevys, a measurable bonus in pride of ownership and immediate status as *the* car expert on your block."

Road Test recorded a quarter-mile ET of 14.0 sec. at 104 mph. In summary, the editors wrote, "If brute power over all other considerations is your forte, the Hemi is still boss on the street and if you'll note what most people put under

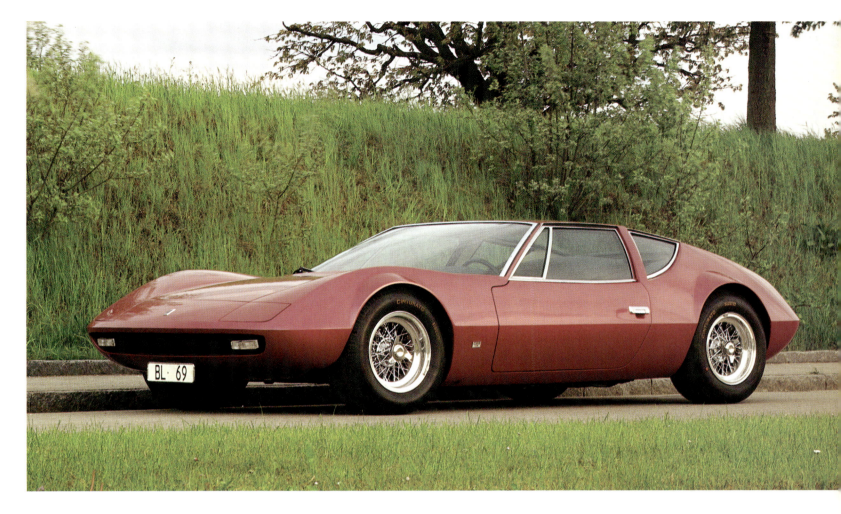

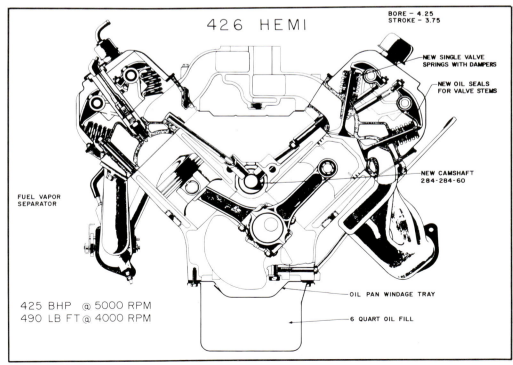

426 HEMI

BORE - 4.25
STROKE - 3.75

NEW SINGLE VALVE
SPRINGS WITH DAMPERS

NEW OIL SEALS
FOR VALVE STEMS

NEW CAMSHAFT
284-284-60

FUEL VAPOR
SEPARATOR

OIL PAN WINDAGE TRAY

6 QUART OIL FILL

425 BHP @ 5000 RPM
490 LB FT @ 4000 RPM

Peter Monteverdi was a Ferrari dealer based in Basel, Switzerland, who decided to construct his own series of sports cars and high-speed limousines. In 1969, he showed the prototype for his ultimate car, a mid-engined sports car built around a 426 Hemi, called the Hai 450 SS. Hai stood for "shark" in German; 450 stood for the horsepower Monteverdi was able to produce from the Hemi. With the mid-engine layout feeding the 490 lb-ft of torque to the rear tires through a five-speed ZF transaxle, the car was reported to accelerate from 0–60 mph in 4.9 sec. and top 175 mph. He planned to hand-build about one car per month, although in the end only three Hai 450 SS cars were constructed. Automobile Quarterly

Chrysler made numerous refinements in the 426 street Hemi for 1968. Chrysler

The 1966 Dodge Charger with optional 426 Hemi had to have muscle to back up its performance styling. You had to look fast to spot the 426 Hemi medallion on the front fenders. Chrysler

For those who wanted a lower profile than a Dodge Charger, you could order your 426 Hemi in a Dodge Coronet 500. This was a 1967 model. Chrysler

a supercharger in Top Fuel Eliminator, it's boss on the strip as well.''

Perhaps the most distinctive Hemi-powered car Plymouth ever built was the Hemi 'Cuda, introduced in 1970. It wasn't a distinct model in the new 'Cuda line that year, but when you ordered the 426 Hemi in your 'Cuda it was identified as such on the standard shaker hood scoop with "hemicuda" on the sides of the scoop. The rear quarter panels received subdued graphics with the word Hemi as additional identification. It was the only Mopar during the 426 Hemi's production between 1966 and 1971 where Hemi was used in the name of the car. Despite being an option in the 'Cuda, the ads for the Hemi 'Cuda gave the implication of being a distinct model.

One ad showed a 1970 Hemi 'Cuda in a field of psychedelic-colored flowers. Then there was the famous Bob Grossman airbrush illustration of the Hemi 'Cuda that appeared as a two-page

spread. The car was shown in caricature, a typical Grossman technique with the accompanying line: "The Rapid Transit Authority." The ad stated, "It's Hemi 'Cuda. Our angriest, slipperiest-looking body shell wrapped around ol' King Kong hisself." Not many supercar ads caught your attention like this one.

End of the Hemi Line

Few enthusiasts could foresee the end of the golden performance car era. Fewer still found out that 1971 would be the last year of the Chrysler 426 street Hemi. Those who read the industry journals learned of this and some of the enthusiast magazines hinted that the end might be near for all high-performance engines, but Chrysler wasn't about to admit it was stopping production of its most famous high-performance engine. Those who did see the handwriting on the wall and knew this would be their last chance to buy a street

When Dodge restyled the Charger for 1968, they also changed the Hemi medallion, dropping the 426. This was a 1969 Charger with optional 426 Hemi. Chrysler

Hemi prudently did so. And there were precious few 1971 street Hemi Dodges and Plymouths built.

Many Mopar enthusiasts in general and Hemi enthusiasts in particular wish they had had the wisdom—and the money—to walk into a Dodge or Plymouth showroom in the fall of 1970 to place an order for a 1971 Hemi-powered car. Better yet, to have ordered two—one to drive and the other to keep in storage with zero mileage, for true investment appreciation. But then, car collecting has always been this way. Certain cars are never thought of as collectible during their day, only years, perhaps decades, later.

Perhaps the most coveted Hemi Mopars in 1971 were the Hemi-powered Challenger and Hemi 'Cuda convertibles. Current owners love stating how few of their particular models were built. In fact, production numbers are some-

times an issue of heated debate and a matter of pride for the Hemi Mopar owner.

This raises the question of just how many 426 street Hemi Dodges and Plymouths were built between 1966 and 1971. Good estimates are between 10,000 and 12,000 cars.

It was perhaps best that Chrysler didn't attempt to put the 426 Hemi through an emasculating emissions certification program, but there were other pragmatic reasons for stopping production in 1971 as well.

"It was a matter of qualifying it for emissions," Tom Hoover says, "and the fact the insurance companies had come down hard on the people who were buying the cars at the time. It was prohibitive to own one, and the market dried up. If I had it to do over again, I would have used my influence to make it a single four-barrel engine in the street version instead of the eight-barrel version that was built."

Changes to the 426 Street Hemi

Throughout its six years of production, the 426 street Hemi's performance remained the same: 425 hp at 5000 rpm

with 490 lb-ft of torque at 4000 rpm. Had it remained in production beyond 1971, it would have suffered the same eventual fate as the other engines in Chrysler's line-up in particular and the auto industry in general. Tightening emissions controls and lower-octane unleaded gas forced the lowering of compression ratios, retarded ignition timing and conservative camshaft profiles. Government legislation of the automobile was forcing the de-emphasis of performance. It did not make fiscal or marketing sense to attempt to certify the 426 Hemi in the face of these realities, and 1971 was chosen as the last year of production.

Despite its steady power ratings over its six years, the 426 street Hemi did receive some modifications. The engine block remained unchanged until 1970, when a new block designed for supercharged and fuel-burning racing applications with heavier main webs and cylinder walls was introduced. According to Chrysler, all Hemi blocks with a casting date on the side of the block after January 19, 1970, had these improvements.

Plymouth introduced a new performance model for 1967—the GTX. The standard 440 ci V–8 could be deleted in place of the optional 426 Hemi. Identifying medallion was different from Dodge. Chrysler

Three different camshafts were used in the 426 street Hemi. For 1966 and 1967, the mechanical-lifter cam had 276 deg. of intake and exhaust duration with 0.46 in. lift. In 1968, Chrysler introduced enough changes to the 426 Hemi to call it Stage II. It included a camshaft with a longer duration of 284 deg. for both intake and exhaust, and a slightly higher lift of 0.47 in. The factory rating of the engine, however, remained unchanged.

Additional changes for the Stage II Hemi included single instead of double valve springs having 279.5 lb. spring pressure at 1.37 in., full rubber umbrella-type valve stem seals instead of the Teflon scraper-type, new Moly-filled piston rings, and a 6 qt. oil pan with windage tray.

In 1970, Chrysler introduced a hydraulic-lifter camshaft having the same specifications as the 1968 and 1969 mechanical cam to reduce maintenance. Interestingly, Chrysler did not do away with the adjustable rocker arms, but retained them. The hydraulic camshaft was carried over for 1971. Due to the new hydraulic lifters, new pushrods had to be designed. New springs were also used having 320 lb. pressure at 1.37 in. This engine is considered by some to be Stage III, and this Hemi is the most troublefree to maintain.

The Elephant Motor Reigns Supreme

Chrysler's decision to stop production with the 1971 model year had long-term positive effects. It retained for the Hemi an image of the ultimate street performance engine; all street Hemis were horsepower kings. Regardless of whether it was a 1966 Charger or a 1971 Hemi 'Cuda, each churned out 425 hp. Consequently, there were no 250 hp 426 street Hemis with anemic camshaft timing, wheezing through a single-exhaust system with catalytic converter.

The largest and most powerful beast to walk the face of the earth is the elephant, and for this reason the 426 street Hemi earned the nickname Elephant Motor. Ceasing production of the street Hemi in 1971 kept it that way. The

The tunnel rear window was used on all 1968–1970 Dodge Chargers except the Charger 500 and the Daytona. The second-generation Dodge Charger was one of the finest performance styling statements of the muscle-car era. Musclecar Review

The restored 426 Hemi of the 1970 B Body Charger R/T. Restoring a Hemi-powered Mopar is exacting work. Chrysler used numerous parts suppliers during the muscle-car era and so there are many variations in components from model to model and year to year. Debate still rages as to what component or finish may be accurate for a given model in a given year. Musclecar Review

This Hemi-powered Dodge Charger has Chrysler's beefy four-speed manual transmission with the terrific pistol-grip shifter. The design for the pistol-grip shifter was the brainchild of Chrysler's Bruce Raymond. For the Mopar enthusiast, it doesn't get any better than this. Musclecar Review

Hemi's bloodlines, so to speak, remained pure, untainted by any emissions-choked evolution.

Chrysler seriously looked into building a big-block for the seventies having Hemi heads with numerous modifications to reduce manufacturing costs and to comply with upcoming emissions standards. Known as the Ball-Stud Hemi to those working on the program, the A279 engine program was intriguing in its concept. The idea was to combine the hemispherical-combustion-chamber cylinder head with current B and RB cylinder blocks. It would feature a new, less-complicated valve actuation using ball-studs at each stamped-metal rocker arm, instead of the forged rocker arm and shaft.

The head-bolt pattern of the B and RB engines was to be retained. To literally get around this problem—the same one encountered when the 426 Hemi was being designed—the intake and exhaust valves were rotated around the hemisphere. This was a necessary compromise to achieve economical valve-train assembly.

The A279 Hemi actually reached the engineering prototype stage and several engines were built. The engines were tested in the dyno labs that were still running tests on the 426 Hemi. Output was disappointing at first, but it soon surpassed that of the 440 V–8, although it stopped short of the 426 street Hemi. This engine could have served a variety of large-displacement applications in Chrysler cars and trucks, without tarnishing the image of the 426 street Hemi, but the corporation decided not to approve production of the A279.

The void left by Chrysler when it ceased production of the 426 would eventually be picked up by the great names in racing engines and, two decades later, by Chrysler Corporation itself.

The owner of this 1970 Hemi Charger R/T chose wider aftermarket wheels to put more rubber on the road. For the stoplight grand prix, this is the way to go. Musclecar Review

Previous page
The 1970 Dodge Charger was the last year of this body design before changing for 1971. When you ordered the R/T, reverse-facing scoops were fitted over the scallops on the doors. No fresh-air hood was optional on the 1968–1970 Charger but one was available on the rebodied Charger for 1971. Musclecar Review

Plymouth released the Superbird in 1970. Based on the Road Runner, it used a similar nose and rear wing as the NASCAR stocker to permit Plymouth to race the car. Richard Petty raced his number 43 Superbird with great success. David Gooley

The standard engine in the Superbird was the Chrysler 440. The 426 Hemi was optional and the original owner of this car obviously made the right decision. No form of fresh-air hood scoop was available on the Superbird. Note the bold 426 Hemi sticker on the air-cleaner cover. David Gooley

The most awesome display of power projection on the street during the sixties was the 1969 Dodge Daytona. It turned heads everywhere it was driven. Chrysler's Larry Rathgeb was the chief engineer behind the wind-tunnel testing that shaped the Daytona. Musclecar Review

Previous page
This Daytona is fitted with the rare optional aluminum wheels. The standard engine was the 440 V–8. When the optional 426 Hemi was ordered instead, a low-key medallion was affixed to the doors between the scallops. Musclecar Review

The interior of the Dodge Daytona was stock Charger. Nevertheless, it made a sporty, elegant statement. The TorqueFlight automatic transmission was superbly engineered to handle the mountains of torque put out by the 425 hp 426 Hemi. Musclecar Review

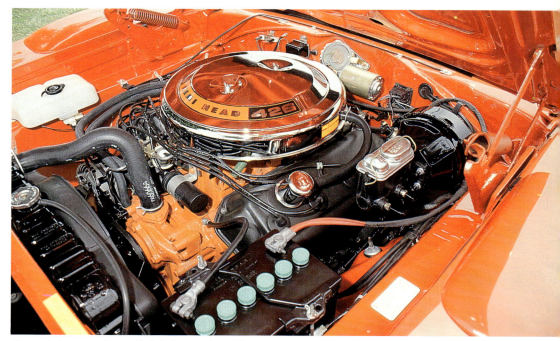

One of the most beautiful sights to the 426 Hemi enthusiast. On those 426 Hemi engines with the chrome air cleaner, this "426 Hemi Head 426" decal was affixed. Musclecar Review

A few Hemi 'Cudas were ordered with the optional factory rear-deck spoiler. This option was really more for show than function. Note the appropriate license plate. David Gooley

Identification under the hood on the Hemi 'Cuda took the form of lower-case letters on the sides of the Shaker hood scoop. It was low-key intimidation of the most subtle kind. Smart drivers pulling up next to one took the hint. David Gooley

In 1970, Plymouth redesigned the Barracuda, and a new era in Mopar muscle cars dawned. The E Body Barracudas and Dodge Challengers were an inspired combination of flowing lines and rawboned beauty. The Hemi 'Cudas took the look to the next stage with the Shaker hood scoop, hood pins, vinyl roof, rear-deck spoiler and hockey-stick Hemi graphics. David Gooley

The interior of the 'Cuda was unquestionably handsome. This car is equipped with the TorqueFlight automatic transmission. Driving a Hemi 'Cuda convertible was the ultimate in top-down cruising. It still is for a privileged few. Musclecar Review

The Shaker hood scoop was a much better system of fresh-air induction than the complex Air Grabber or Ramcharger designs on other Mopars. Here the Shaker has been removed, exposing the dual four-barrel carburetors with their staged linkage. Musclecar Review

The Ford Mustang launched the pony-car era in Detroit, but the most handsome embodiment of the period has to be the 1970 Plymouth Barracuda. The performance version was simply called 'Cuda. When the option 426 Hemi was ordered, it became the Hemi 'Cuda. Musclecar Review

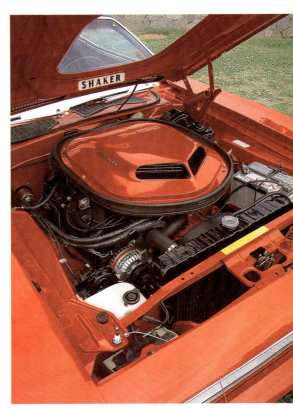

Chrysler designed what was probably the best-looking hood scoop in the industry to go on its high-performance 'Cudas and Dodge Challengers. Chrysler coined the name Shaker for its hood scoop—and shake it did, particularly on top of the 426 Hemi. David Gooley

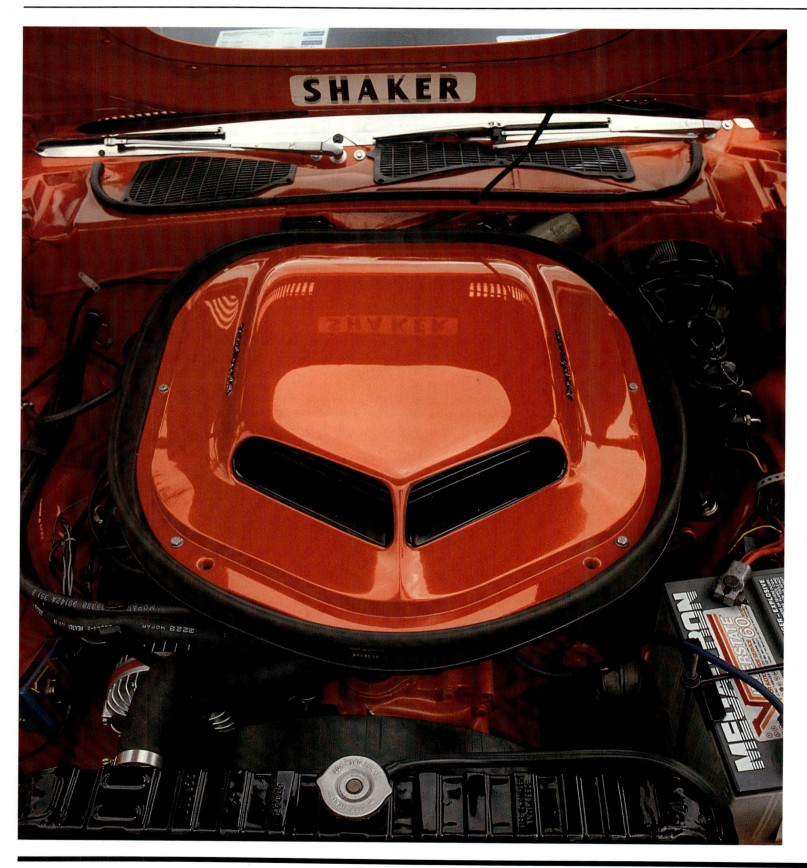

The Hemi Today

The Elephant Engine Lives On

The guy who has a Hemi race car sitting in his garage as well as the guy who has a Hemi car for restoration—this is where we obviously knew we had a market and that's why we did it.

—Larry Shepard

Through the sixties and seventies, both the first-generation Hemi and the 426 Hemi continued to be the most successful engines used in sanctioned drag racing. This continued success motivated aftermarket companies to offer parts for the 392 and 426 Hemi engines. Eventually, it became economically feasible for some firms to offer aluminum-block versions, and these engines took on new life.

Ed Donovan

During the 1950s, many racers felt the 392 Hemi was the best thing to ever happen to the sport. Despite being designed as a passenger-car engine, the largest first-generation Chrysler Hemi was horsepower-maker supreme. Many manufacturers produced parts for use with the 392 and its popularity continued into the sixties.

One of the true believers in the 392 Hemi's virtues was Ed Donovan. He had raced Ford flatheads in the forties. Later, he gained valuable engine-design experience working for Offenhauser. He continued racing and was drawn to drag racing in particular. He saw the need for stainless-steel valves that could endure the rigors of racing, and began machining them at home. Slowly, he branched out, making other parts, which con-

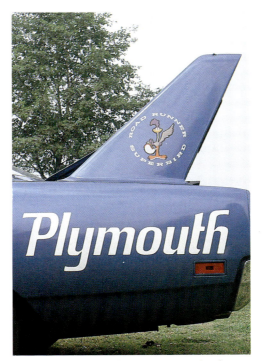

The Plymouth Road Runner Superbird was Plymouth's answer to Dodge's Charger Daytona, and again only a small number were fitted with the 426 street Hemi, above. Left, the Shaker hood scoop on a 1970 Hemi 'Cuda. Emissions controls and noise-limit regulations would doom such performance, but the Hemi lives on in the 1990s. David Gooley

sumed more of his time. In 1957, he left Offenhauser and opened Donovan Engineering to devote full time to his burgeoning business.

Racing was always the vehicle for producing and testing his parts to prove their durability and performance. In 1962, Donovan built a 270 ci blown Offenhauser dragster that reached 186 mph in the quarter-mile. Still, the small Offy was never designed for such applications, and Donovan looked to the big American V–8s for inspiration.

The Chrysler 392 Hemi had become a popular engine to use in drag racing, and Donovan produced parts for this engine to meet the demand. Despite the advent of the Chrysler 426 Hemi in 1964, the 392 Hemi continued to be a popular engine on the quarter-mile strip. Donovan felt the 392 Hemi could be improved upon but the cost of doing so was, at first, prohibitive.

By the end of the sixties, Donovan's performance parts business had grown rapidly, matching the explosion of drag racing's popularity. With his resources and manufacturing capability, Donovan could realistically consider filling a need for a truly durable engine based on the 392 Hemi head but designed strictly for drag racing. Donovan had been harboring the dream of designing an aluminum

A full-tilt Keith Black aluminum 426 Hemi is capable of churning out thousands of horsepower. Keith Black

engine block that embraced the advantages of the 392 while eliminating its weaknesses. It had to be able to withstand the fearsome stresses imposed by the use of nitromethane, the most powerful and volatile fuel used in drag racing. With so many stock and racing parts available for the 392 Hemi, a racer could literally build a strong racing engine around the new block Donovan had designed.

Donovan spent countless hours with his small design and manufacturing team before the block configuration was finalized, and work began in 1970. All major dimensions—deck height, camshaft centerline to crankshaft centerline, and bore-to-bore centers—were retained. Bore diameter, however, was increased from 4.00 to 4.125 in., boosting displacement to 417 ci. Instead of being a solid block, it was an open-block design using centrifugally cast chrome-moly steel wet-sleeve liners. The result was a much lighter yet stronger block, and the sleeves were interchangeable and easily replaceable. This design made it possible to develop greater horsepower than was possible before.

The second major component of the engine was the main bearing girdle, also of aluminum, that provided massive support to the crankshaft. In the stock 392 Hemi, this was a weakpoint from a racing standpoint. This new bottom-end in conjunction with the new block permitted almost unrestricted application of supercharging with nitromethane fuel.

Together, the aluminum block, girdle and steel cylinder liners tipped the scales at just under 200 lb. Steel studs were used throughout the engine to permit repeated teardown and reassembly without galling otherwise tapped holes.

Donovan's chief engineer, Bob Mullen, produced the drawings for the engine. Arnold Birner made the precision wood patterns for the block, girdle and cylinder liners. Dick Crawford established the tooling requirements for drag racing's first aluminum engine block.

After the casting and machining procedures unique to the Donovan 417 were worked out, the engine was offered to eager drag racers in 1971. The engine made its debut at the NHRA Super-Nationals in John Wiebe's rail, setting a low ET for the racers of 6.53 sec.

Proof of the 417's viability and durability is the fact the engine is still manufactured and sold today. Donovan went on to offer an aluminum 350/400 small-block in 1978. He followed this with an aluminum-block 427/454 in 1983.

When Ed Donovan died of cancer in May 1989, his wife Kathy became head of the company, continuing the long-standing Donovan Engineering reputation.

Keith Black

In Keith Black's office is a book that he has been working on for years. It's titled: "All I Know About Racing Engines." Inside, all the pages are blank. It's always good for a laugh, and it says a great deal about the man.

"I'm not a writer," Black says. "I'm a doer."

The name Keith Black is known to thousands of drag-racing enthusiasts as one of the sport's finest engine designers and builders. In a sport and profession that is fiercely competitive, he has remained uncompromising and forthrightly honest.

He was born in Lynwood, California, in 1926. Like many other teenagers in southern California, he became interested in hot rodding while in high school during the early forties. After graduating, he entered the Army Air Corps cadet program but World War II ended before he was called to action.

He married his high school sweetheart and set about the task of making a living in the postwar economy. Early on, he displayed an uncanny ability repairing and hot-rodding engines. His career actually started with boats, not cars. It all began when a friend asked him to fix the carburetor problems in his boat. A hobby became a career, and he started working out of his backyard.

"As I became successful at it," Black says, "more people would come to me and ask, 'Would you work on my engine?' I worked on a few Cadillac and Oldsmobile engines because they were the first ones out [with V–8s]. The first time I got into a race deal, where I had something that was of some size, I went into a Chrysler Hemi because I felt the engine was more of a race engine than the rest of the engines were. At that time, I did engines for boat racing that were 246 cubic inches, from the small Dodge [Hemi] engine. We built those up fuel-injected—some of them methanol. We also did a 265 cubic inch DeSoto."

As his business grew, he moved to Atlantic Avenue in South Gate, California. Black continued building boat racing engines into the early sixties, setting new national and international records every year. In 1965, Bob McCurry took over the Marine and Industrial division of Chrysler. McCurry learned of Keith Black's skill in building marine racing engines and flew out to California to meet with him.

"He came out and met me in my shop," Black recalls, "and he said, 'OK, I want to do for marine racing what Holman and Moody did for Ford, and I want you to do it.' We started in 1966 in the program to develop the late Hemi engine. Bob McDaniel was my immediate boss at Chrysler who worked for McCurry."

In the latter part of 1966, Black was called to help sort out the problems experienced by the twin-engine, Hemi-powered *Miss Chrysler Crew.*

"McDaniel said, 'Build up six engines, get started now. We'll start next year,'" remembers Black. "We built the engines and in 1967 we maintained the engines, went with the boat during the year and we ended up with second place in high points for the year."

In June 1967, Black moved to larger facilities on Scott Avenue in South Gate. It proved good timing because his involvement with the Hemi was about to grow dramatically.

"At the same time," Black continues, "I was told to make the late Hemi run as a fueler. Well, we put Barry McCown in the hospital from his drag boat at the time and it scared me. I said, 'You know, it's tough to develop these things in the boats because of trying to find a place to run them and all the things that are involved. I can do it much quicker in a car.' Bob McDaniel said,

The Chrysler Hemi continues to be the engine of choice in Top Fuel drag racing. Gene Snow shows what Mopar performance is all about. Thompson Advertising

'Then do it!'

"So we did the *Hawaiian II,* driven by Mike Sorokian. In fact, it said Chrysler Marine across the top of the rocker covers. The *Hawaiian I* ran a 392 Hemi. We did the development work on the *Hawaiian II* until it was far enough along where we did away with the second car. We put the [426 Hemi] engine in the primary car and we never looked back. By that time, the end of '67, Dale Reeker was my boss, but Bob McCurry started it all. McCurry came to me with the confidence to get the job done, and I thank him to this day for the opportunity."

The end of production of the 426 Hemi was a key event in the creation of the Keith Black aluminum 426 Hemi. The other key event was the arrival on the drag-racing scene of the Donovan 417.

"We had talked about an aluminum Hemi and I presented it to Chrysler but they looked at it and said, 'Well, we don't think there's any point in us building an aluminum Hemi. We're in the business of building cars.' And I had to agree. I couldn't argue with them, so we never did anything.

"Finally, Donovan built an aluminum early [392] Hemi. They took it to the racetrack and ran the thing. They announced it over the loudspeaker and called it the Donovan aluminum engine. All the guys around me who said they couldn't afford it started ordering it. I thought, 'These guys tell me they can't afford it and they're ordering it. That means that's baloney. They'll buy whatever they've got to have.' So I sat down and decided to make a late Hemi.

"So, I went to work on it. Bob Cahill at Chrysler called me and said, 'Did you know that Don Alderson is building a late Hemi also?' So I called Don, because we knew each other and talked about it. But he knew what he wanted to do and I knew what I wanted to do, so we both did it. The only thing was, it took me three years; it took him about a year. I did it [that way] because I couldn't afford it and nobody was paying for it but me. So I paid for it as I went.

"When I told them (Chrysler) I was going to make an aluminum Hemi, they said, 'Fine. Can we help you?' And I said, 'Yes, what can you do for me?' And they said, 'Anything that doesn't cost money.' So I said, 'Send me the current drawings for the Hemi, so I'll have that to work from for dimensions.'

"In the meantime, Alderson had his out in the marketplace and sold some.

Hemis have been used in Funny Cars ever since the 1965 A/FX cars Chrysler built—the original cars that coined the classification. A Hemi gives the Hawaiian Punch *Dodge Daytona* its punch. Bruce Biegler

We'd even put some together for some of our customers. Then we came out with our part. There was both of us in the market, then pretty soon he was gone."

Black initially encountered difficulties in finding a foundry that could produce a high-quality aluminum block. He visited two foundries, but found they couldn't do the job to his satisfaction. Then, through a pattern maker, he learned of another place that had the capabilities to do the job. He started offering his aluminum 426 Hemi block in 1974.

He followed this by offering cast-iron Hemi cylinder heads because of his desire to run on nitromethane, but Black says he could never make the iron heads work successfully on nitro. He switched to aluminum heads, but the foundry couldn't produce heads up to the quality he wanted, so he took over this operation himself.

Thanks to the 426 Hemi's incredible success on the drag strip over the decades, Keith Black expanded the list of parts available for his Hemi where today

he sells everything from the intake scoop to the oil pan.

"Our business has been mostly motivated by people wanting something," he says, "or we knew needed something and we'd make it. I started out making nothing and finally ended up making everything!"

Mopar Performance

Today, Mopar enthusiasts view the passing of the 426 Hemi as a milestone. As with most milestones in automotive history, the former glory of a particular car or engine remains just that. When Chrysler struggled to cope with the emissions and safety standards in the seventies and reorganization and rebuilding the corporation in the eighties, performance was not a major issue in the product offerings. Seeing the return of the iron-block Chrysler 426 Hemi was as plausible as turning water into gold.

Implausible perhaps, but not impossible. Certain events occurred in the late eighties that made the prospect of Chrysler offering the venerable 426 iron block to Mopar enthusiasts a serious possibility.

When Larry Shepard joined Chrysler in 1966, the reputation and popularity of the 426 Hemi were growing dramatically. In 1970 he moved to the race group and concentrated on drag racing. Chrysler received many requests for information regarding the 426 Hemi as well as their other engines, and per-

formance tips from both professional and amateur racers alike. Shepard worked alongside Dave Koffel, who handled the professional racers; both men reported to Tom Hoover.

"Back in those days," Shepard remembers, "Koffel worked with the contract racers, but they didn't have someone for what we'd call the 'door slammers'—someone to coordinate with our customers who had questions. Koffel would receive countless letters asking questions concerning performance, and there weren't enough hours in the day to handle them."

That job fell to Shepard. He began sifting through the filing cabinets full of letters with questions and began sorting them according to their specific query. These covered the gamut, from each of Chrysler's engines to the cars themselves. He also fielded phone calls with promises to get back to them with an answer. Koffel would often direct him to the engineer with specific knowledge regarding the performance area in question. Shepard felt he should never have to ask any question twice, and always wrote down the information. He began cataloging the answers to questions and putting them into binders. Still, this was far from ideal.

It occurred to Shepard that it would be more practical to write a bulletin in a given area and send that in response to a query, rather than responding to each letter or phone call individually. He began writing technical bulletins addressing key performance issues that were most frequently asked and originally these bulletins were given away. Later, the bulletins were sold through the Hustle Stuff parts catalog. Eventually, these bulletins were compiled into one book and sold through Chrysler's Direct Connection parts catalog. This book grew to such a size, it was decided to split it and publish two books, one for engines and the other for chassis.

In 1987, the Direct Connection name was changed to Mopar Performance. This name was readily identifiable by every enthusiast and tied in with existing parts sold by Chrysler. With the name change came the mandate to emphasize hard parts —the parts Mopar enthusiasts wished to buy—such as engine blocks, cylinder heads, intake manifolds, crankshafts, pistons, camshafts and so on.

"Looking back over our shoulder," Shepard says, "that decision has allowed us to become more visible in the performance marketplace and opened the door to very large dollars to allow capital-intensive programs."

At drag races around the country and such events as the Mopar Nationals, the Mopar Performance traveling display always draws crowds. Shepard never misses these events because it keeps him in tune with the enthusiasts who use Chrysler products. He began hearing complaints on the scarcity of 426 Hemi blocks and the outrageous prices that were being asked. Many of these blocks were more than twenty years old and had seen hard use. Additional demand was placed on the market by restorers of street Hemi cars, and those simply interested in putting a 426 Hemi in their Dodge or Plymouth or in a custom street rod.

The resurging interest in the 426 Hemi led Shepard to the conclusion that Chrysler should offer the 426 Hemi iron block to meet this demand.

"The guy who has a Hemi race car sitting in his garage as well as the guy who has a Hemi car for restoration—this is where we obviously knew we had a market and that's why we decided to do it."

The decision to reissue the 426 Hemi iron block was the biggest commitment Mopar Performance has ever made in terms of dollars and in overcoming some serious obstacles.

"The Hemi tooling was lost many years ago," Shepard admits, "so we would have to go back and make the tooling all over again. We've built up slowly up to this point, making intake manifolds, crankshafts, camshafts and so forth. Our goal at Mopar Performance was to be able to build a Hemi engine from top to bottom from our parts catalog. Will having Hemi parts change the way people think about the Hemi? We think so."

With its firm decision to reissue not only the 426 Hemi iron block but also cylinder heads and every part needed to build a complete engine, Chrysler has ensured its most famous V–8 will be available to Mopar enthusiasts for generations to come.

Appendices

1948–1971 Hemi Prototypes and Production Engines

A161
This was the 1947 Hemi-head research and development test engine with a Hemi head added to a straight-six Chrysler engine.

A182
The 1948 Chrysler 330 ci Hemi V–8 prototype.

A239
The 1948–1950 331 ci Hemi V–8 prototype that became the Chrysler FirePower engine. Shorter and lighter than the A182.

A864
The 426 race Hemi V–8, developed initially in 1963–1964 by adding a Hemi head to a raised-block 426 ci engine.

A925
Prototype 1964 426 race Hemi with four valves per cylinder and double overhead camshafts.

A990
Drag-race lightweight 426 Hemi developed initially in 1964 using aluminum-alloy cylinder heads and other alloy parts as well as a cast-magnesium intake manifold.

A117
Circle-track 404 ci race Hemi developed initially in 1966 based on the A864 426 race Hemi but using a shorter, 3.558 in. stroke.

A148
Prototype 1965–1966 426 race Hemi based on the shorter, 3.558 in. stroke of the A117 but with a larger 4.363 in. bore and larger valves. Aluminum-alloy and iron cylinder heads were experimented with, as was a gear-driven camshaft and a flat crankshaft.

A102
The 426 street Hemi, initially developed in 1965.

A103
The 426 Stage II street Hemi, initially developed in 1967–1968.

A279
The Ball-Stud Hemi 440 ci big-block prototype initially developed in 1968 as a low-cost challenger to Chevrolet's big-blocks. Ball studs were used instead of the forged rocker arms, and the Hemi heads were added to a 440 ci Chrysler block. Program was canceled in 1970.

Chrysler FirePower Specifications

	1951 FirePower	1957 FirePower	1958 FirePower EFI
Displacement (ci)	331	331	392
Bore (in.)	3.81	3.81	4.00
Stroke (in.)	3.63	3.63	3.90
Compression ratio	7.5:1	8.5:1	10.0:1
Horsepower	180 @ 4000	300 @ 5200	390 @ 5200
Torque	312 @ 2000	345 @ 3200	435 @ 3600

Dodge Red Ram Specifications

	1953 Red Ram
Displacement (ci)	241
Bore (in.)	3.44
Stroke (in.)	3.25
Compression ratio	7.1:1
Horsepower	140 @ 4400
Torque	220 @ 2000

DeSoto FireDome Specifications

	1952 FireDome	1957 FireDome
Displacement (ci)	276	345
Bore (in.)	3.63	3.80
Stroke (in.)	3.34	3.80
Compression ratio	NA	9.25:1
Horsepower	160 @ 4400	345 @ 5200
Torque	NA	355 @ 3600

426 Hemi Comparative Specifications

	1964–1965 Track	1966 Track	1964 Drag	1965 Drag	1966 Street
Displacement (ci)	426	426–404	426	426	426
Bore (in.)	4.25	4.25	4.25	4.25	4.25
Stroke (in.)	3.75	3.75–3.558	3.75	3.75	3.75
Compression ratio	12.5:1	12.5–12.0:1	12.5:1	12.5:1	10.25:1
Cylinder block	Cast iron stress relieved	Cast iron stress relieved	Cast iron stress relieved	Cast iron stress relieved	Cast iron stress relieved
Bearing caps	Mall. iron tie bolted	Mall. iron tie bolted	Mall. iron tie bolted	Mall. iron tie bolted	Cast iron tie bolted
Crankshaft	Forged steel shot-peened and nitride-hardened 0.015 in. journals	Forged steel shot-peened and nitride-hardened 0.005 in. journals	Forged steel shot-peened and nitride-hardened 0.015 in. journals	Forged steel shot-peened and nitride-hardened 0.015 in. journals	Forged steel shot-peened and nitride-hardened 0.015 in. journals
Main bearings	Trimetal	Trimetal	Trimetal	Trimetal	Trimetal
Main journal diameter (in.)	2.75	2.75	2.75	2.75	2.75
Crankpin diameter (in.)	2.375	2.375	2.375	2.375	2.375
Piston	Impact extruded aluminum	Impact extruded aluminum	Impact extruded aluminum	Impact extruded aluminum	Impact extruded aluminum
Piston weight (gm)	852	813	852	848	843
Top of skirt to bore clearance (in.)		0.008			0.003
Piston pin offset (in.)	0.060 toward minor thrust side	0	0.060 toward minor thrust side	0.060 toward minor thrust side	0.060 toward major thrust side
Piston pin					
OD (in.)	1.0936	1.0936	1.0936	1.0936	1.0311
ID (in.)	0.751	0.750. S6 taper	0.751	0.751	0.685
Type	Pressed	Floating	Pressed	Pressed	Floating
Connecting rod	Forged steel	Forged steel	Forged steel	Forged steel	Forged steel
Centers	6.861	7.061 426 7.174 404	6.861	6.861	6.861
Intake valve	Silchrome XB	Silchrome XB	Silchrome XB	Silchrome XB	Silchrome XB
Head diameter (in.)	2.25	2.25	2.25	2.23	2.25
Stem diameter (in.)	0.309 solid	0.309 solid	0.309 solid	0.309 solid	0.309 solid
Stem finish	Chrome	Chrome	Chrome	Chrome	Chrome
Exhaust valve	21–4N	21–4N	21–4N	21–4N	21–4N
Head diameter (in.)	1.94	1.94	1.94	1.94	1.94
Stem diameter (in.)	0.308 solid	0.308 solid	0.308 solid	0.308 solid	0.308 solid
Stem finish	Chrome	Chrome	Chrome	Chrome	Chrome
Valve springs installed height					
Outer (in.)	1.86	1.86	1.86	1.86	1.86
Inner (in.)	1.64	1.64	1.64	1.64	1.64
Valve closed load					
Outer (lb.)	85	85	85	85	105
Inner (lb.)	40.5	40.5	40.5	40.5	50
Valve open load					
Outer (lb.)	280	288	272	280	184
Inner (lb.)	94	96	92	94	91
Wire size					
Outer (in.)	0.216	0.216	0.216	0.216	0.187
Inner (in.)	0.128	0.128	0.128	0.128	0.128
Water pump body	Cast iron	Cast iron	Cast iron	Cast iron	Cast iron
Impeller diameter (in.)	3.32	3.32	3.67	3.67	3.67
Water pump housing	Cast iron	Cast iron	Cast iron	Aluminum	Cast iron
Oil pump body	Cast iron	Cast iron	Cast iron	Aluminum	Cast iron

	1964–1965 Track	1966 Track	1964 Drag	1965 Drag	1966 Street
Oil pump cover	Cast iron with cooler tubes	Cast iron with cooler tubes	Cast iron	Aluminum	Cast iron
Oil suction pipe	Dual-fixed and swinging	Dual-fixed and swinging	Single	Single	Single
Intake manifold type	Aluminum conventional single 4 bbl	Aluminum plenum-ram single 4 bbl	Aluminum plenum-ram dual 4 bbl	Magnesium plenum-ram dual 4 bbl	Aluminum two-level tandem 4 bbl
Manifold heat	None	None	None	None	Exhaust gas
Exhaust headers	Steel casting and tubes	Plate and tubes	Steel casting and tubes	Plate and tubes	Cast-iron manifolds
Carburetors	Single Holley	Single Holley	Dual Carter	Dual Holley	Dual Carter
Choke			Manual	Manual	Automatic hot air
Rod bolts (in.)	7/16–20	1/2–20	7/16–20	7/16–20	7/16–20
Bolt load	0.008/0.0085 stretch	0.0095/0.010 stretch	75 lb-ft	75 lb-ft	75 lb-ft
Cylinder head	Cast iron machined hemisphere	Cast iron machined hemisphere	Cast iron machined hemisphere	Aluminum machined hemisphere	Cast iron machined hemisphere
Chamber radius (in.)	2.42	2.42	2.42	2.42	2.42
Chamber depth (in.)	1.34	1.34	1.34	1.34	1.34
Chamber volume (ci)	172.7	172.7	172.7	170.4	172.7
Camshaft	Hardenable cast iron	Hardenable cast iron	Hardenable cast iron	Hardenable cast iron	Hardenable cast iron
Cam sprocket attachment	Single 7/16–14	Three 3/8–16	Single 7/16–14	Single 7/16–14	Three 3/8–16
Timing chain	Double roller	Double roller	Silent	Double roller	Double roller
Intake duration	312	328	300	312	276
Intake max. open	112 ATDC	106.5 ATDC	114 ATDC	112 ATDC	106 ATDC
Exhaust duration	312	328	300	312	276
Exhaust max. open	112 BTDC	109.5 BTDC	110 BTDC	112 BTDC	114 BTDC
Overlap	88	112	76	88	52
Intake valve lift (in.)	0.54	0.565	0.52	0.54	0.48
Exhaust valve lift (in.)	0.54	0.565	0.52	0.54	0.46
Rocker ratio					
Intake (in.)	1.57	1.57	1.57	1.57	1.57
Exhaust (in.)	1.52	1.52	1.52	1.52	1.52

D Series 426 Race Hemi Cylinder Heads

D1
Alternate cylinder heads for the 426 race Hemi initially developed in 1969 using the same intake and exhaust valves but with larger exhaust valve ports.

D2
Alternate cylinder heads for circle-track racing initially developed in 1969 with a 0.02 in. overbore giving 429 ci.

D3
Alternate cylinder heads for the 426 race Hemi initially developed in 1969 using larger intake and exhaust valves.

D3.5
Alternate cylinder heads for the 426 race Hemi initially developed in 1969 using the larger intake valves and ports of the D3 and larger and straighter exhaust ports of the D4.

D4
Alternate cylinder heads for the 426 race Hemi initially developed in 1969–1970. It used the same intake valves and ports as the D1 but with larger area, higher exit and straighter exhaust ports.

D5
Alternate cylinder heads for the 426 race Hemi initially developed in 1970 with all of the improvements of the D4 but cast in aluminum alloy and using two spark plugs for each cylinder.

D20 Magna
Alternate cylinder heads for the 426 race Hemi initially developed in 1970 with substantially larger ports and a wider iron head to house the ports.

D21 Magna
Alternate cylinder heads for the 426 race Hemi initially developed in 1970 as an aluminum-alloy version of the D20 Magna.

426 Street Hemi Specifications

Engine

Type	90°V
Number of cylinders	8
Bore	4.250 in.
Stroke	3.750 in.
Compression ratio	10.25:1
Piston displacement	426 ci
Engine output:	
horsepower	425 hp @ 5000 rpm
torque	490 lb-ft @ 4000 rpm

Combustion chamber specifications

Combustion chamber volume	168 cc min.; 174 cc max.

Distance from top of piston to block deck	0.502 to 0.547 in.
Maximum variation between cylinders	30 psi

Cylinder numbering

Left bank	1–3–5–7
Right bank	2–4–6–8

Cylinder block

Material	Tin-alloyed cast iron
Cylinder bore	4.250 to 4.252 in.
Cylinder bore finish	0.020 to 0.035 in.
Tappet bore diameter	0.9050 to 0.9058 in.

Intake manifold

Material	Cast aluminum
Type	Double level

Crankshaft and main bearings

Type	Forged counter-balanced, shot-peened and chemically treated (hardened journals)
Bearings	Tri-metal—copper–lead alloy with steel backing (MS–2355)
Diameter main bearing journal	2.7495–2.7505 in.
Diameter crankpin	2.374–2.375 in.
Clearance	0.0015 to 0.0025 in. (selective fit)
End play	0.002 to 0.0085 in.
Finish at rear seal surface	Diagonal knurling
Interchangeable bearings	Lower nos. 1, 2, 4, 5
	Upper nos. 2, 4, 5
Main bearing bolt torque	100 lb-ft
Main bearing tie bolt torque	45 lb-ft

Connecting rods and bearings

Rods:	
Type	Drop forged I-beam
Length	6.861 in.
Weight (less bearing shells)	1084 gm
Bearings:	
Type:	Tri-metal—copper–lead alloy with steel backing (MS–2355)
Diameter and length	2.376x0.927 in.
Clearance	0.0015 to 0.0025 in.
Side clearance (two rods)	0.009 to 0.017 in.

Camshaft

Drive	Double roller chain
Bearings	Steel-backed Babbitt
Number	5
Thrust taken by	Cylinder block
Clearance	0.001 to 0.003 in.

Camshaft bearings

Journal diameter (mean)	
No. 1	1.9985 in.
No. 2	1.9825 in.
No. 3	1.9675 in.
No. 4	1.9515 in.
No. 5	1.7485 in.
Bearing clearance	0.001 to 0.003 in.

Timing chain (Special roller type)

Adjustment	None
Number of links	66
Pitch	⅜
Width	0.86 in.

Valves—intake

Material	Silicon-chrome XB
Head diameter	2.25 in.
Stem diameter	0.309 in.
Stem to guide clearance	0.002 to 0.004 in.
Angle of seat	45°
Lift	0.460 in.
Duration	276°
Lash (cold)*	0.028 in.

*Due to the high overlap, long duration and high lift of the camshaft, special care must be taken to be sure each tappet is on the base circle of its cam lobe when clearance is set.

Valves—exhaust

Material	21–4N chrome-manganese with welded stellite face
Head diameter	1.94 in.
Stem diameter	0.308 in.
Stem to guide clearance	0.003 to 0.005 in.
Angle of seat	45°
Lift	0.460 in.
Duration	276°
Lash (cold)	0.032 in.

Valve springs

Number	16 (inner); 16 (outer)
Free length	2.20 in. (inner); 2.47 in. (outer)
Installed height	1.83 in. min.; 1.89 in. max.
Load when compressed:	
Valve closed:	
inner	47–53 lb. @ 1.635 in.
outer	102–108 lb. @ 1.86 in.
Valve open:	
inner	86–96 lb. @ 1.175 in.
outer	179–189 lb. @ 1.40 in.
Valve spring diameter (outer)	1.090 in.
Surge damper	Spiral type

Tappets

Type	Mechanical
Clearance (in block)	0.0010 to 0.0023 in.
Body diameter	0.9035 to 0.9040 in.

Pistons

Type	Domed forged aluminum

Material	Extruded aluminum alloy, tin-coated
Clearance at top of skirt	0.0025 to 0.0035 in.
Weight	843 gm

Piston rings

Number of rings per piston	3
Compression	2
Oil	1
Ring side clearance	
Top compression	0.0015 to 0.003 in.
Second compression	0.0015 to 0.003 in.
Oil ring (steel rails)	0.0002 to 0.005 in.

Cylinder head

Material	Cast iron
Combustion chamber	Hemispherical
Valve seat run-out (maximum)	0.002 in.
Intake valve seat material	Integral
Intake valve seat angle	45°
Intake seat width	0.060 to 0.080 in.
Exhaust valve seat material	Integral
Exhaust valve seat angle	45°
Exhaust seat width	0.05 to 0.07 in.
Cylinder head gasket material	Stainless steel
Cylinder head gasket thickness when compressed	0.025 in.
Cylinder head bolt torque	70–75 lb-ft*

*Uses new, special hardened cylinder head bolt washers.

Engine Lubrication

Pump type	Rotary full pressure
Capacity	5 qt. (add 1 qt. with filter change)*

Pump drive	Camshaft
Oil pressure	1000 rpm to 8 psi (hot) 45–65 psi (cold) @ 40–50 mph
Oil filter type	Full-flow

*Check oil level indicator (dipstick) and change if necessary to correspond to correct level. Maintaining proper oil level is necessary during acceleration trials.

Fuel pump

Type	Mechanically operated, diaphragm type
Pressure	6–8 psi

Carburetor

Type	Two, 4-bbl. downdraft
Model	AFB-4139S front AFB-4140S rear
Throttle bore	
Primary	1 7/16 in.
Secondary	1 11/16 in.
Main venturi	
Primary	1 3/16 in.
Secondary	1 9/16 in.
Idle speed (engine hot)	750 rpm
Idle mixture (both screws open)	1–2 turns

Ignition system

Distributor type:	Double breaker, automatic advance
Basic timing	12° BTC
Advance— centrifugal (crankshaft degrees @ engine rpm)	0° @ 1000 rpm 9° @ 1400 rpm 17° @ 2800 rpm
Advance automatic— vacuum (distributor degrees @ inches of mercury)	0° @ 6 to 9 in. 4.5 to 7.5° @ 12 in. 8.25° to 11° @ 15 in.
Breaker point gap	0.014 to 0.019 in. (use dwell meter for final setting)

Dwell angle	
One set points	27 to 32°
Both sets points	37 to 42°
Breaker arm spring tension	17 to 21.5 oz.
Rotation	Counterclockwise
Spark plugs	
Type	N–9Y
Size	14MM 3/4 in. reach
Gap	0.035 in.
Firing order	1–8–4–3–6–5–7–2
Coil	PN 2444242 PN 2444241
Primary resistance @ 70–80°F	1.65–1.79 ohms 1.41–1.55 ohms
Secondary resistance @ 70–80°F	9,400–11,700 ohms 9,200–10,600 ohms
Ballast resistor Resistance @ 70–80°F	0.5–0.6 ohms
Current draw (coil and ballast resistor in circuit)	
Engine stopped	3.0 amps
Engine idling	1.9 amps
Clutch	
Free-play adjustment	1/2 in. min.; 3/4 in. max.
Rear axle	
Axle shaft end clearance	0.13 in. min.; 0.023 in. max.
Ratio	3.23 automatic 3.55 manual
Torqueflite transmission	
Line pressure	90 psi @ 1000–1100 rpm
Oil (engine)	Only oils labeled "For Service MS" should be used. Note: SAE 30 is recommended for acceleration trials
Transmission fluid	
Manual	SAE 80–90 gear oil
TorqueFlight	Use automatic transmission fluid Type A suffix A
Capacities—transmission	
Manual— four-speed	7 1/2 pt.
TorqueFlight	18 pt.

Index

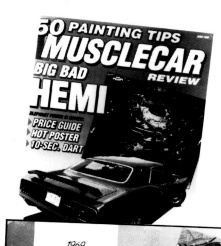